GANDHI
THE DAWN OF INDIAN FREEDOM

Owing to the antiquity and rarity of this book, certain pages are regrettably absent, and readability is compromised due to the blurring of the original text. If you possess any insights regarding the availability of these missing sections, kindly inform us. Your assistance is crucial in ensuring the completion of this significant work for the benefit of future generations.

GANDHI
THE DAWN OF INDIAN FREEDOM

VERRIER ELWIN

GYAN

Published by

Gyan Publishing House
5, Ansari Road
Daryaganj, New Delhi-110002
Phone: 011-47034999, 9811692060
E-mail: books@gyanbooks.com

Distribution Network
gyanbooks.com
India, USA, Canada, UK, Australia

ISBN: 978-93-7447-101-2 (PB)

2nd Impression 2026

Printed at: Gyan Press, Delhi.

GANDHI THE DAWN OF INDIAN FREEDOM
Author: VERRIER ELWIN

GANDHI:
THE DAWN OF INDIAN FREEDOM

by

JACK C. WINSLOW

and

VERRIER ELWIN

NEW YORK CHICAGO

Fleming H. Revell Company

LONDON AND EDINBURGH

VANDE MATARAM

HAIL to thee, Mother! Thy proud sons greet thee,
  Fair as the moon and clear as the sun;
Terrible fair as a bannered army;
  Patient and strong till the day be won;
Calling thy sons to the high endeavour;
  Sealing them true to the task begun.

Others will fight with hatred and slaying,
  Wade to a kingdom through blood outpoured.
We will conquer with God's own armour;
  We will slay with the Spirit's sword;
Vanquish by Love that can meekly suffer;
  Die and arise in the name of the Lord.

Prophet souls that have watched for the dawning,—
  Patient hope in your sleepless eyes,—
Cry and exult! for the flags of morning
  Flame on the face of the eastern skies!
Welcome the end of your night's long travail!
  See your sun in his strength arise!

India, my India! Mother beloved!
  Shatter the chains of thy thraldom past!
Ransom thy captives and raise thy fallen!
  Fold to thy bosom thy sons outcast!
Rise in the might of thine ancient splendour!
  Shout for thy great Release at last!

J. C. W.

FOREWORD

There is always difficulty in establishing mutual understanding between Englishmen and Indians. Our natural habit of mind is profoundly different, and we are liable on each side to attach to phrases used on the other meanings that were not intended. For this reason, as well as for many others, I have been one of those who have watched with deep sympathy and hopefulness the enterprise known as Christa Seva Sangha.

It is a brotherhood composed of Englishmen and Indians, living together according to Indian customs, founded with the object of interpreting the Christian Gospel to India in the utmost possible detachment from the purely European or British elements, which inevitably tend to cling to the preaching and exposition of it by those whose habit of thought has been moulded by Western philosophy.

In the turmoil of recent years it has been inevitable that the members of this brotherhood should come to certain conclusions about the conditions which must be fulfilled if good will, peace and happiness are to prevail in India; and so it has come about that two men who have given their lives to interpret the Christian Gospel to India have felt an obligation resulting from their experience to interpret the Indian mind to England at this time. I am not in a position to form any opinion of value with regard to the estimate they set forth concerning political movements or problems, but as a friend of Christa Seva Sangha I wish to commend to my own fellow-countrymen a book which may be fruitful in creating a truer appreciation of the Indian outlook than many of us are likely to receive from utterances either of Indians or of Englishmen who have not had this peculiarly intimate association with Indians.

That we should understand is the first requirement. I wish to make it clear that I am neither commending nor criticizing the contents of this book otherwise than as a contribution to the English understanding of the Indian mind. But for this, which is the first necessity, I believe that it has a peculiar value.

WILLIAM EBOR

CONTENTS

INTRODUCTION

The eyes of the world are to-day focussed upon India, watching intently the outcome of that country's efforts to attain *Swaraj*. With an even closer intentness they are focussed on the figure of the man in whom India's will for freedom finds unique embodiment, and on whom her destiny in a supreme measure depends. It is no exaggeration to say that during the fateful fortnight of Mahatma Gandhi's negotiations with Lord Irwin the whole world waited with breathless interest to know what the result would be. Not only was the scene of the "half-naked fakir," just released from prison, conferring as ambassador of all India with the Viceroy dramatic in a high degree, but it was realized that far more than the future of India depended on the outcome of that conference. It is with the same realization that the world is awaiting the result of the resumed Round Table Conference in London.

The writers of this book are both Englishmen who have thrown in their lot with India and desire to serve her. In what they have written they have endeavoured to interpret something of the Indian outlook to the West.

The first chapter deals with the imminent attainment of freedom by India, and gives reasons why such a prospect should arouse, not so much fears of the disastrous consequences which may follow the coming of *Swaraj*, as hopes of the contribution which emancipated India may make to the world's advance.

The second chapter gives a picture of the man in whom the spirit of India has taken visible shape, and who was the outstanding figure at the London Conference. It does not attempt to give his story, which is now well-known, but tries, with the help of some personal experiences and of some of the Mahatma's more recent writings and utterances, to add some fresh touches to a portrait now in its main outline familiar to the world.

The third chapter is concerned with the most fundamental and the most central of Gandhi's teachings,—that of *Satyagraha*. It seeks to expound its meaning with some detail and exactitude; to illustrate its use from the different campaigns in which it has been made the principal weapon; and to discuss its value as a "moral equivalent for war."

The last chapter starts from the assumption that, whether we like it or not, India will in the near future be a free country, and seeks to estimate the part which the Christian Church should play in this free India, and the conditions essential to her successfully fulfilling that part.

Such a book as this will arouse in some places the indignant query, "Why should two Christian priests spend their time writing on politics? Is not religion their proper sphere? And would it not be much better if they kept to it?"

It is of some importance that the answer to this query should be properly understood.

We should, therefore, say at the outset that we

have not written merely on politics as such. The purely political issues we have left on one side. We have not, for instance, attempted to discuss whether the launching of the Civil Disobedience Movement in 1930 was wise or unwise; whether a federation is the best form of constitution for a united India; nor any of the details concerning the proposed new constitution. We have been concerned, rather, with the great moral and spiritual issues underlying recent political events in India, or inevitably involved in her future development. And the consideration of such issues seems, on several grounds, to be a task which all Christians are free to undertake.

In the first place we maintain that the religion of the Incarnation is bound to claim the whole of human life as its province. That Incarnation has consecrated with the Divine Presence every aspect and department of our common life. The Christian can say, in a deeper sense than the Roman philosopher, "*Homo sum; nihil humanum a me alienum puto.*" We cannot, without being false to our creed, regard any great human issue as outside the sphere of religion.

This has always been realized by the Christian Church, and it is scarcely necessary to recall the part played in political affairs by great Christian saints, such as Bernard of Clairvaux and Catherine of Siena. The encyclical of Pope Leo XIII, *Libertas Praestantissimum,* made clear the Church's traditional attitude to politics, and to political liberty in particular—"It is expedient to take part in the administration of public affairs. And the Church approves of everyone devoting his services to the common good, and doing all that he can for the defence, preservation, and prosperity of his country. Neither does the Church condemn those who, if it can be done without violation of justice, wish to make their country independent of any foreign or despotic power. Nor does she blame those who wish to assign to the State the power of self-government, and to its citizens the greatest possible measure of prosperity. The Church has always most faithfully fostered civil liberty."

Of recent times the far-reaching obligations of Christian citizenship have been freshly realized, and the great C.O.P.E.C. Conference at Manchester only brought to a head a movement which had for many years been acquiring strength. We understand to-day, as perhaps never before in the history of the Church, that Christianity covers the whole of life, and every aspect of existence must come beneath its sway. Politics, especially in their international and racial aspect, are not exempt. The recent Lambeth Conference declared that "Peace will never be achieved till international relations are controlled by religious and ethical standards," and that "peace within the nation and among the nations is bound up with the acceptance of Christian principles in the ordering of social and industrial life." Again, it says, "As citizens of the kingdom of God we are summoned to make war on injustice, falsehood, and covetousness within ourselves and in the world around us. Neither industry nor commerce nor finance lies outside the borders of the kingdom of God, for at every point they touch human values and depend on human motives, and nothing human is alien to Him who came that men might have life and have it abundantly."

The Church in India has been slower than the Church in England to realize the truth of this position. The newer attitude represented by the C.O.P.E.C. Conference seems only very inadequately to have filtered through. Too often in India we hear it said that Christianity has nothing to do with politics. Government, for its own purposes, has encouraged such an attitude. It has insisted on a pledge by all non-British missionaries that they will take no part in political matters. It has only refrained from exacting a similar pledge from British missionaries because it regarded them as allies; and, in cases where British missionaries have ventured to take an independent line, it has sought to bring pressure to bear upon them through the ecclesiastical authorities.

Thus missionaries in India have, with very few exceptions, refrained from bringing their religion to bear upon political issues, and Indian Christians, in this as in other matters, have in the past been too ready to follow the missionary lead. The inevitable result has been to produce the impression on the minds of Indians generally that they could look for little sympathy with their national aspirations from the Christian Church, and that the missionaries in particular were either the servants of the Government, or at least unable and unwilling to take any action which Government might disapprove.

This impression is specially disastrous in a country where the new gospel of fearlessness and the duty of every man, and especially the man of religion, to follow truth regardless of consequences has caused a moral revolution.

It is therefore a matter of special importance in India that we should stand up at all costs for the right, and indeed the duty, of Christians to play their part in public affairs, and to apply the principles of the gospel to every branch of economic, civic and national life.

If further justification be needed for our writing on these matters, we would urge that the Church of the West has a right to demand that those whom she has sent to India, and who have had special opportunities of judging Indian problems near at hand, should give her the benefit of their experience in the forming of her own judgments. Christians of the West are bound to study the great issues facing the world, and England in particular, to-day in connection with the Indian political situation. They will wish to reach right convictions upon them—convictions consonant with the principles of Christ. To whom should they look to help them in forming such convictions if not to those in India who are both their fellow-countrymen and their fellow-Christians?

But, whether our action be approved or not, we cannot be silent. Great issues for the Kingdom of God are hanging in the balance, and no man who has a zeal for the Kingdom can remain aloof or indifferent. We have sought to approach the Indian question from the standpoint of religion. It is a question peculiarly amenable to such an approach. Religious issues are woven into its very texture. And we have sought to show what we believe the Church's duty to be in view of the new situation that faces her at this dawn of Indian freedom.

The authors will probably be criticized for giving too enthusiastic and one-sided a picture of the Indian situation. In common with the Indian Nationalist leaders they are fully aware of the many civic and social evils which India shares with other nations. But these have already been given, often in an exaggerated form, so much publicity that the authors have not cared to dwell on them.

It only remains to thank the Archbishop of York for finding time, in the midst of his manifold labours, to show his sympathy with our undertaking by writing a foreword.

Our thanks are due to the "Friends of India" Association, 46 Lancaster Gate, London, W. 2, for their assistance in the publication of this book.

The two authors have indicated the chapters written by them respectively, and desire to state that, while they are in general agreement with one another, neither is committed in detail to the views which the other has set forth.

Their hope is that, by God's blessing, what they have written may be of service for the Kingdom of God and for the beloved motherland of their adoption.

Royalties received by the authors from the sale of this book will be devoted to the work of the Aundh Ashram of the Christa Seva Sangha, a village Ashram devoted to the uplift of the poor.

J. C. W.
H. V. E.

NOTE
TO CHAPTERS II AND III

For the facts and quotations given in Chapters II and III I am indebted primarily to the files of *Young India*, Mahatma Gandhi's own paper, which is the living mouthpiece of his thought. I have also used among others the following books which may be consulted by those who wish to explore the subject more exhaustively: Among Mahatma Gandhi's own writings—*My Experiments with Truth; Satyagraha in South Africa; Self-Restraint versus Self-Indulgence*. For the events in South Africa, I have also consulted *Speeches and Writings of M. K. Gandhi*. A full account of Champaran Satyagraha is given in Rajendra Prasad's *Satyagraha in Champaran*. The Bardoli Movement of 1928 is vividly described by Mahadev Desai in *The Story of Bardoli*. For the 1930 Civil Disobedience Movement, I have consulted, in addition to periodical and newspaper files, the eighth edition of Natesan's publication, *Mahatma Gandhi: the Man and his Mission*, and *The Black Regime at Dharasana*, which described the raids on the salt-depots. Those interested in the philosophy of Satyagraha should possess R. B. Gregg's *The Psychology and Strategy of Gandhi's Non-violent Resistance*. Mr. C. F. Andrews's *Mahatma Gandhi's Ideas, Mahatma Gandhi: His Own Story*, and *Mahatma Gandhi at Work* offer, for Western readers, the most penetrating and sympathetic account of the Mahatma's thought.

These chapters have gained in accurate presentation through the help of Sjt. A. V. Thakkar and Dr. B. N. Khambata. I received some valuable suggestions from Bhai Gurdial Mallik and Sjt. Jamshed Mehta; and I would express my gratitude to Srimati Ala Pocha for placing her unrivalled collection of "Gandhi Literature" at my disposal.

Some paragraphs in Chapter II appeared originally in *The Bombay Chronicle*, from which they are reproduced by permission of the Editor.

V. E.

THE DAWN OF INDIAN FREEDOM

CHAPTER I

THE GANDHI-IRWIN PACT AND AFTER

I

The conclusion of the agreement between Mahatma Gandhi and Lord Irwin on March 4, 1931, was, both in itself and in its consequences, an event of outstanding importance.

In itself it was a triumph of spiritual forces. The two leaders, it was widely recognized, achieved something to which the term "miracle" could not inappropriately be applied. It was a victory (not of one side but of both), won by the weapons of faith and goodness, or (as Gandhi himself put it) by "the principles of the Sermon on the Mount." The effect produced was profound. The fact that the destinies of two great and rival nations happened, for the time at least, to be in the hands of two profoundly religious men, both convinced of the supremacy of the forces of the Spirit, revealed, on a scale which circumstances seldom render possible, the power of faith to remove mountains. It is difficult to exaggerate the moral and spiritual significance of the pact.

Its consequences are of no less vital importance. It has done something towards dispelling the clouds of racial animosity and distrust which had so long darkened the Indian horizon, and has made it possible for Mahatma Gandhi himself (still the outstanding force in Indian politics) and for the Congress (the overwhelmingly predominant party in Indian nationalism) to co-operate in the Round Table Conference, in the hope that it may be possible to reach the goal of Indian freedom by the way of mutual agreement rather than by the way of further conflict and strife, whether violent or non-violent.

The entry of Mahatma Gandhi and the Congress into the Round Table Conference meant that India's claim to complete *Swaraj* was pressed with even more uncompromising vigour than in 1930. This may make it more difficult for agreement with the various British parties to be reached, for there will undoubtedly be widely divergent views needing to be reconciled; but, on the other hand, a most powerful incentive to arrive at a settlement will be provided by the knowledge that, on the one hand, such a settlement, if reached, will be accepted by practically the whole of India, and that, on the other hand, the failure of Britain to meet India's claims will be followed by civil disobedience of an intensified character, enacted on a nation-wide scale, and not easily to be curbed within the restraints of non-violence. The position is thus critical in an exceptional degree; and it is clear that the future, not only of India, but of the British Empire, and in some measure of the whole world, turns upon the issue of the Conference.

The writers of this book make no claim to be politicians, and it is not their business here to discuss in detail the political issues which will arise in the Conference. But, as Englishmen nurtured in the traditions of freedom, they cannot but be profoundly stirred by India's struggle for liberty and supremely eager that England should respond with unstinted generosity to India's claim. "No Englishman," said Lord Irwin in a speech made shortly before leaving India, "can, without being false to his own political history, and in recent years to his own pledges, take objection to the pursuit by others of their own political liberty."

One would have supposed *a priori* that all Englishmen would share these sentiments. It ought not, one would think, to be necessary to argue with an Englishman the case for freedom, since his whole training has led him to realize that freedom is a nation's birthright; that foreign domination, however efficient and beneficent, rankles in the hearts of all patriotic citizens, not merely because it wounds their self-respect, but because it destroys initiative and free self-expression, induces a "slave mentality," and kills the nation's soul. Yet it is unfortunately true that there is still a considerable section of English people who are unwilling to apply to India the principles on which they would insist for their own country, and who demand that India should still remain under British domination.

I am not here concerned with those whose motives are purely selfish,—those who maintain with Lord Brentford (though they may not always express their views so frankly as he) that England occupied India for her own material advantage and that she must continue to hold it from the same motive. That is an honest and intelligible position which cannot be refuted except by arguments which will induce a complete change of moral outlook.

But there remains a considerable number of English people, of high moral character and real desire for India's welfare, who are sincerely convinced that for India's own sake Great Britain ought to retain a strong hold upon the country, and that the gift of freedom would be the betrayal of a sacred trust. They point to certain disastrous results which would inevitably follow if India were to be given real independence at the present time. These fears and anxieties deserve careful consideration.

I need not deal with the fear that India will be left at the mercy of foreign invaders, as the retention of a British army large enough for defence against foreign invasion is one of those temporary safeguards which the country is willing to accept in her own interests, while an adequate Indian army is being trained.[1]

A fear expressed by many well-wishers of India is that under *Swaraj* internal chaos will prevail. Each community will fight for its own hand; bribery and corruption will increase; real justice will be impossible; nepotism will be widely prevalent.

With regard to this sombre anticipation several things may be said.

First this. The different communities in India

[1] I ought, perhaps, to add that this statement must not be taken to imply that the writers of this book approve of the employment of military force.

already for the most part live amicably together. There are large areas of the country, for instance, in which Hindu-Moslem strife hardly ever breaks out. Where there is real rivalry and bitterness, it is only suppressed, not cured, by British intervention. You cannot make two opponents love one another by standing between them and preventing them from flying at each others' throats. India, like other countries, must learn to work out her own salvation. No doubt there will be quarrels,—perhaps serious ones. But I cannot believe that the communal problem is really so difficult of solution. Amongst the younger men it hardly exists. The national bond is for them so strong that it overrides communal differences. The influence of the older and more orthodox sections, among whom the differences are more acute, is already waning. The leaders everywhere are striving hard, and with considerable success, to achieve national unity. I see no likelihood of anything happening in India comparable to the chaos and anarchy which has been the lot of China.

Then in regard to bribery and corruption and the maintenance of justice the same general principles will apply. The imposition of *British* justice (which in itself is not infallible, specially where racial issues are concerned) does little to encourage the growth of *Indian* justice, so long as responsibility is lacking. One can only learn justice by having the chance to exercise it. And I see no reason to doubt that a free India will realize the importance of high standards of integrity in public life and set herself progressively to achieve them.

As to nepotism, is British public life free from this even now? It is not so very long ago since it was rife even within the Church.

In regard to all these matters we have to remember that a dependent nation has very little incentive to reform itself. It tends to leave reforms to be carried out by the Government. But, if India secures her freedom, the sense of self-respect that will come to her, and her new position among the other free nations of the world, will compel her to set her own house in order and reform abuses in her public life. The amazing discipline exhibited by most of the Congress volunteers during the Satyagraha struggle, a discipline to which one of the provincial Governors has borne generous testimony, is a happy foretaste of the loyal co-operation which the leaders of a free India may hope to secure from the people in all efforts to build a sound and stable commonwealth. I believe myself that the standard of public life in India will compare favourably, under *Swaraj*, with that of most other countries.

A second anxiety expressed by English well-wishers in regard to *Swaraj* is that it may be, not a real democracy, but the tyranny of a Brahmin oligarchy over the masses. In reply to this it must be said that the "masses" are becoming rapidly more and more capable of looking after their own interests. Already in the Madras Presidency, covering the greatest part of South India, non-Brahmins are politically stronger than Brahmins, and it is the Brahmins who will suffer, if any community does, under Home Rule. The non-Brahmins of other parts of the country are quickly following suit and realizing that they have only themselves to blame if through lack of education they are not wielding the influence to which their numerical superiority would otherwise entitle them. Even the various outcaste communities are now asserting their rights with no uncertain voice, and their claims are being increasingly heard; and it should be remembered in this connection that some of the strongest advocates of the abolition of untouchability have been Mahatma Gandhi himself and his followers in the Congress, and that, if they should come into power, they will certainly see that the rights of the outcastes are secured.

It has also to be borne in mind that the young and ardent spirits who form the various Youth Leagues of the country, and who under leaders like Pandit Jawaharlal Nehru are likely to determine the trend of India's development during the next generation, are definitely committed to the policy of the uplift of the masses and the abolition of social inequalities. In fact, it may be asserted with some confidence that, if the prophetic vision of our anxious foreboders of evil extended somewhat further, the real menace of the future which would haunt their imaginations would not be that of Brahmin tyranny but that of a communism in which all aristocracies have been wiped out of existence.

For all these reasons, then, there are no very solid grounds for fearing that Home Rule in India will mean oppression of the masses by a Brahmin oligarchy. This might have been so some years ago, and it is natural that those Englishmen whose contacts with India have been of an earlier date should still cherish these anxieties. But the day of the Brahmin's monopoly of power is over, and it is probable that, for the short period during which the now illiterate classes may still need protection, safeguards will be provided for them in the new constitution.

I must now deal with two fears which have been not infrequently expressed by Christians interested in the progress of the Christian Church in India.

The first is that, under *Swaraj*, the striking "mass movements" of outcastes and others into the Christian Church will be, if not arrested, at least diminished in intensity. It is pointed out that the prestige of Christianity as the religion of the ruling race has been a not unimportant influence in the mass movements. Missionaries as members of the ruling race have been regarded as persons of influence, whose protection and help could do much to uplift the community. If the Government of the country ceased to be Christian in name, one of the powerful motives for joining the Christian Church would be removed.

The answer to this is not difficult to see. Conversions based on, or influenced by, such considerations of prestige or worldly advantage are, we are bound to maintain, not genuine conversions; and, in so far as the mass movements are relying on such adventitious aid, it can only be for the good of the Christian Church that they should be arrested and purified.

My own belief is that the true progress of the Gospel will be greatly assisted by the grant of real independence to India. If the prestige of belonging to the religion of the rulers has been an inducement to the outcastes to join the Christian Church, it is equally (or even more notably) true that the association of Christianity with the ruling race has been a hindrance to its real understanding and acceptance by Indians of education and standing. But at least the disappearance of even the nominal identification of the rulers of the country with the Christian religion will clarify the whole issue as to what the acceptance of Christ means, and will put an end to the taunt and the fear that it involves a failure in true patriotism. A thoughtful Hindu has lately written: "But for India's subjection to Western imperialism many more in India would rejoice in the name of Jesus," and it can be safely said that many others would be found to echo his sentiments.

The other fear expressed by those who are specially concerned for the advance of the Church in India is that under *Swaraj* the Christians may have to suffer persecution, either directly or by the many indirect methods in which persecution can be made effective.

My answer to this would be that, in the first place, direct persecution is unlikely so long as Christians are playing a useful part in the national life and helping forward national progress; and that, in the second place, if there should be persecution, whether direct or indirect, the Church, so far from being injured by it, will be greatly purified and strengthened. If, for instance, a law were passed forbidding all efforts to win converts to Christianity, and the Church offered civil disobedience in the spirit of Mahatma Gandhi's *satyagraha* campaign, can we doubt that it would have for Christians the same effect which this campaign has had, unifying and purifying them and giving them new zeal and courage? The blood of the martyrs has always been the seed from which new life has sprung; and we need not doubt that it would prove to be so once more in India.[1]

These, then, are the answers which I should myself give to the various fears expressed about the consequences of giving India her freedom. Troubles, mistakes and difficulties there will be, perhaps of a serious character. Only through such travail pangs can the new India come to the birth. But what is the alternative? Is it some further years of quiet tutelage by Great Britain and a continued gradual advance to self-determination along the lines of the Simon Commission Report? All who know India must surely realize by now that this is impracticable. No Indian party, however moderate, would be willing to work such a constitution. No, the only alternative that remains to the grant of real liberty is (as I have said above) the renewal of strife on an enlarged scale, the attempt to carry out yet more drastic but fruitless repression, and at last the enforced surrender to India of her freedom and a long heritage of bitterness, instead of its voluntary bestowal now and a long heritage of friendship. Can we doubt which course to choose?

[1] This matter is dealt with more fully in Chapter IV.

II

But, if once we are convinced that the time has come for Britain to give India the substance of independence (whether because of our own enthusiastic faith in freedom, or because we are forced to recognize that no other course is now practicable), then fears and anxieties for the future may well give place to hopes based upon the vision of what an India really set free for self-expression and self-development might give to the world. Instead of concentrating our attention on the dangers inherent in India's attainment of *Swaraj*, we shall do well to dwell on some of the gains which it should bring. For it is evident that the best energies of large numbers of India's ablest citizens have for some years past been put into the effort to secure India's freedom, and that, when that task has been accomplished, those energies will be set free for other forms of constructive work, which cannot be without their fruit.

I must not here assume the rôle of the prophet, and attempt to forecast in detail what the future development of a free India may be. But a few broad generalizations may perhaps be allowed.

It can safely be anticipated that a far larger percentage of the revenue than now will be devoted to education, and there will be a great increase of literacy. We may hope to see a larger development of such completely Indian centres of education as that of Rabindranath Tagore at Shantiniketan. We may also expect a great encouragement of indigenous industries, and a sustained effort to relieve the poverty of the masses. The enforcement of total prohibition will probably be amongst the earliest measures passed by a free Indian parliament. Some interesting experiments may be expected in the administrative sphere, particularly in the direction of developing local government along the lines of the old *panchayats*.[1] The achievements of Sir Jagadish Bose give some foretaste of what Indian brains may be able to achieve in the sphere of scientific research.

But for my own part I believe that it will be in the moral and spiritual sphere that a free India will make her greatest contribution to the world's wealth; and I would illustrate this in relation to three issues of outstanding importance.

The survival of modern civilization, whether in the East or West, depends upon whether a way can be found to eliminate war as a means of settling international disputes. It is generally acknowledged that a war upon the scale of the Great War of 1914–1918, intensified by all that more recent discoveries have done to make war yet more deadly, would deal that civilization a blow which might well prove fatal. The world's hope rests upon the success of the forces making for peace. Now in the movement for the reduction of armaments and the elimination of war there can be little doubt that the influence of a free India would tell powerfully for peace. In spite of the military reputation of the Sikhs and the Marathas it is, I think, true to say that the Indian

[1] Village councils, consisting normally of five leading men.

temperament is strongly pacific. The principles of non-resistance, of overcoming evil by good, as enunciated in the Sermon on the Mount, meet with wide acceptance. They are implanted deep in the Indian tradition, and have become still more securely rooted through the teaching and work of Mahatma Gandhi. The anarchical movement in favour of violence has not gained any strong hold upon India, and is in any case due to conditions which the establishment of *Swaraj* will end. Thus we may confidently hope that India, when once through independence she has been enabled to make her own voice heard in the councils of the nations, will lend effective aid to the world-forces making for peace.

A second danger which threatens to engulf modern civilization is the worship of wealth. All unprejudiced observers must be ready to admit that the cult of luxury and comfort is developing with alarming rapidity, and threatens, if unchecked, to usher in an era, not only of moral and spiritual, but also of intellectual decadence. I cannot speak from my own experience about any other Western country except England; but on recent visits to England from India I have been greatly struck, not only by the clear evidences of this increasing mammon-worship, but also by the way in which, all over the country, thoughtful people are looking for the birth of some new movement of simplicity of living and protest against luxury, similar to the Franciscan Movement of earlier days, as the one hope of stemming the tide of national decay.

Now, if this demand for a return to simplicity does really represent a need that is widely felt, then once again powerful reinforcement may surely be expected from a free India. In spite of a certain hold which it must be admitted that present-day materialism has gained upon the country, it remains broadly true that India has never worshipped at the shrine of mammon. The glitter of the world's gold has done little to blind her spiritual vision. She has paid her formal tribute to worldly potentates, but she has always reserved her truest homage for the Sadhu, for the man of holy and simple life, whose secret power is the renunciation of all that the world counts dear. No small part of the amazing spell which Mahatma Gandhi still exercises over India is due to his identification of himself with the poorest of the land. Of all the Christian saints it is the Poverello of Assisi who makes to India the tenderest appeal. We may be sure, therefore, that in the struggle against the material forces which threaten to sap the higher life of the nations, India, if she can attain an emancipation which will give her natural genius free scope, will lend assistance which may well prove to be of decisive importance.

More serious even than the menace of militarism and the menace of materialism, because lying at the roots of both, is the menace of secularism. The forces of secularism, all the world over, are gathering intensity year by year. It is becoming increasingly evident that, so far as the issue of religion is concerned, the struggle will be, from now onwards, less a struggle for the victory of one religion over another than a struggle of all who believe in God and in the supremacy of spiritual values against those who would overthrow all religion. Now it is true that this world-wide warfare against religion has invaded India also, and that it is not without its influence, specially amongst the younger generation. But for my own part I cannot but believe, with Rabindranath Tagore, that the Indian is "incurably religious." No other people, except perhaps the Jews, have given to religion so fundamental a place in the whole scheme of life. That Spirit is the one reality is, for India, a truth that hardly needs assertion. And I cannot believe that even the powerful attack of modern secularism will be able to shatter this fundamental conviction of the Indian heart. In comparison with the teeming multitudes of those who believe in God, whether amongst the literate or illiterate classes, an atheist is still rare in India; and when you meet him, he is quite different from the atheist (or at least the blatant atheist) of the West. He has indeed rejected the beliefs and practices of traditional religion, but he has a delicacy of spiritual intuition and a sensitiveness to spiritual influences which one cannot easily associate with "the fool" who "says in his heart 'There is no God.'"

I believe, for my own part, that India will continue to be the home of religion, a land in which religious values count supremely; and that, therefore, in the great Armageddon between God and His adversaries which this century must surely witness, India will bring "to the help of the Lord against the mighty" spiritual battalions which, in this struggle also, may turn the day. Yet in this, as in the other instances, she can only do so if her soul escapes from the fetters which foreign domination imposes upon it, and is free to be *itself*.

There seems, then, good reason to hope that the great spiritual revival for which Christians of the West are waiting may take birth from India. May it not be that Indian teachers and sages will recall us to forgotten meanings and values of our own faith? Narayan Vaman Tilak, the Christian poet of Maharashtra, prophesied of this:

> Yea, at the end of pregnant strife,
> Enthroned as *guru*[1] of the earth,
> This land of Hind shall teach the worth
> Of Christian faith and Christian life.

I submit, then, that hopes like these of what a liberated India might contribute to the world's highest progress, in the critical days which lie ahead of us, may well replace the fears which many feel about the bestowal of *Swaraj*, and enlist even the doubting among the advocates of India's full and effective freedom.

[1] Teacher.

CHAPTER II

THE HALF-NAKED FAKIR

"Mr. Winston Churchill said that it was alarming and nauseating to see Gandhi—late Inner Temple lawyer, now a seditious fakir—striding, half-naked, up the steps of the Viceregal Palace to parley on equal terms with the representative of the King-Emperor."—*The Daily Mail.*

I

The claim and right of India to freedom, discussed in the previous chapter, finds its loftiest and most vigorous expression in the person of Mahatma Gandhi. He is at once the living representative and the chief inspiration of the Indian Renaissance. "In all his transcendent simplicity," says Mrs. Sarojini Naidu, "he is the embodied symbol of the Indian Nation—its living sacrifice and sacrament in one." He may be buried in jail, he may hide himself in the retirement of his Ashram, he may be taken to the utmost ends of the earth, "but his destination remains unchanged in the hearts of his people, who are both the heirs and the stewards of his matchless dreams and his matchless deeds." He is India: he blends in himself her old culture and her new ideal. From time to time men arise who express the very spirit of their age. Such a one is Mahatma Gandhi. The pure and generous idealism which is flowing afresh in the ancient veins of India pulses in his heart. To tell his story is to write the history of the spiritual awakening of the East.

Mahatma Gandhi is without doubt the greatest man now living in the world. "Since Tolstoy died," says Mr. H. N. Brailsford, "there is no human being living to-day who commands as he does the veneration of mankind. Others are liked, respected, and admired, but he stands on a Mount of Transfiguration." To his own intense distress, he is hailed already as an incarnation. There are few parallels in modern history to the crowds which flock to have his *darshan.* He is regarded as having initiated a new era. The old dark age—the *Kali Yuga*—is over: a new age of hope and freedom has begun. To-day we are in the Year 2 of the Gandhi Era. In India his influence—spiritual, moral, social, political—is supreme. The magic of his personality, and the convincing nobility of his ideals, removes all opposition. Again and again he has been made virtual Dictator of India. At Karachi in 1931, he was able to carry an unpopular policy in spite of the discontent and opposition of many of his followers. He was the sole mouthpiece of the Indian National Congress at the London Conference. India, the mother of saints, was proud to be represented at the capital of the British Empire by a half-naked fakir. Many other delegates were present, but they did not express the spiritual heart of India. Only Gandhi could do that.

II

The personality of Mahatma Gandhi is of one piece with his teaching. He is the very embodiment of the

Spirit of Truth, Purity, and Love—the three ultimate values of his philosophy. His life of renunciation speaks to the inmost soul of India. He is one of the few perfectly disinterested men that have walked this earth. You may disagree with his policy: you may even violently oppose it, but you cannot say that he is going to get anything out of it for himself. His self-forgetfulness is the secret of his self-possession and his humble self-confidence. He is conscious of his mission and therefore he has no fear. He has conquered fear, as he has conquered lust and pride and ambition.

He is the incarnation of moral energy. His teaching has that quality of enthusiasm which is a test of truth. There is a vitality and power in his simple words which is more convincing than the most finished rhetoric.

He is not an orator; he has the power of arranging ideas rather than words; yet the effect of his speeches is electrical. He is not a bookish man, but he conveys the impression of a deep and liberal culture. He is no mere visionary: he is a shrewd practical politician, with an extraordinary wide knowledge of human nature. But he is so dominated by his sense of spiritual realities that nothing can shake his optimistic faith in the efficiency of spiritual methods and the ultimate triumph of spiritual ideas.

In the realm of politics, he has simplified the issues and directed attention to the primary human needs of India. He is interested in politics as a school, not of constitution-making, but of character-building. He has created a new public morality.

He has introduced into human politics, says Romain Rolland, the strongest religious impetus of the last two thousand years. Above all, he has brought the ideal of generosity into politics. The very foundation of his Satyagraha is a sort of quixotic chivalry. He is always anxious to meet his opponents and to understand them. He has proved that in public life saintliness is not only practicable but necessary.

In the realm of morals, he has again concentrated on the great human needs. He has built his ethical system not on the dead rock of scripture and scholastic traditions but on the living authority of sincerity and truth. His claims on the conscience of his followers are indeed exalted, but they are clear and lucid, and there is no doubt as to what he demands. He has not only raised a moral standard for the whole nation, but he is the spiritual director of countless individual souls, whose needs he has constantly in mind.

In the realm of religion, like all Indian thinkers, he is dominated by the idea of unity. He believes in the fundamental oneness of all things, and therefore of all religions. This is the philosophical root of his toleration. It is the basis of his tender love of all created things, of which his advocacy of cow-protection, his sympathy with such things as tree-worship and the veneration of images, is an expression. His religion appears to be marked by the fervour and devotion of a Wesley, but modified by the restrained simplicity and dignity of the Catholic tradition of saintliness. His ideal of religion is perhaps a new thing in India. He is freer of dogmatic Hinduism than the prophets of the Ramakrishna Mission: he has a wider and more vital message than the great Brahmo-Samajists: he is less other-worldly than the ancient mystics. Unlike the Vedantists, he has no interest in metaphysics for its own sake.

If we are to compare him to the familiar figures of the West, we may say that in his love of poverty he resembles Francis of Assisi, in his social vision he reminds us of F. D. Maurice, in his sincerity of Tolstoy, in his intellectual integrity of J. H. Newman, in the generosity of his international ideal of Romain Rolland.

He is in no sense a Puritan: he is an ascetic, but an ascetic of the Catholic type. He can combine the romance of life with its renunciation. "Only those capable of life are also capable of God; only those capable of romance are capable of holiness." Child of the seashore and of the desert, there is a strong vein of poetry and romance in his soul. He has a deep love of natural beauty. He delights in the scenery of Ceylon and Travancore, and the snow-white glories of the Himalayas. He writes enthusiastically of Cape Comorin, "where the sea daily washes in adoration the feet of *Hind Mata* (Mother India)." He says again, "When I admire the wonders of the sunset or the beauty of the moon, my soul expands in worship of the Creator." Music also sings to his heart. "Music has given me peace. . . . It has helped me to overcome anger." He never wearies of hearing the melodious recitation of the

Bhagavadgita. Music deepens his insight into truth. He is a real lover of art, provided that Art is the true expression of the soul. Like many of the Catholic saints, however, he feels that the objects of sense-perception have only a relative value. "The outward has no meaning to me at all except in so far as it helps the inward." Beautiful things "would be hindrances if they did not help me to think of God. Anything which is a hindrance to the flight of the soul is a delusion and a snare."

Indeed, in many ways, the teaching of Gandhi illuminates and recalls to the modern world the half-forsaken ideals of Catholic Christendom. Intellectually a rationalist, temperamentally and in the field of ethics Gandhi reveals the closest kinship to Catholicism. He understands and advocates the monastic ideal, in the Franciscan and Jesuit interpretation of it. He knows the power of Poverty. He believes in Celibacy "as practically the only way to realize the beatific vision of God." "It is celibacy," he has said, "that has kept Catholicism green up to the present day." His own practice of fasting and silence links him to the great Catholic saints. He has written enthusiastically about his visit to a Trappist monastery in South Africa. Nor is the counsel of Obedience alien to him—the fidelity to rule, the sacrifice of the will, the perfect surrender to God, the "intense longing to lose myself in the Eternal, and become merely a lump of clay in the Potter's divine hands, so that my service may become more certain because uninterrupted by the baser self in me." He believes in Penance. He told the priests of the great Temple at Pandharpur, "The Himalayas are spotlessly snow-white in virtue of the spotless glory of the countless sages who laid down their lives performing penance in their caves. Only such penance can save us and our religion from perdition to-day."

His love of prayer, his stress on discipline, his desire that religion should be ordered and reasonable, his pre-eminent belief in the supremacy of spiritual values, mark him as a saint of the Catholic (and in some respects of the mediæval) type.

This chapter will not attempt to record the story of Gandhi's life, which he himself has told with such engaging frankness, nor will it give a complete picture of his teaching. It will simply try to penetrate to something of his secret, to describe certain aspects of his spiritual teaching, and to give some account of the moral and spiritual revolution that he has effected.

I believe that the real secret of Gandhi's power is his Franciscanism—that the same sort of things which made men love Francis are making men love Gandhi, his poverty, his self-control, his humility, his joy, his sympathetic kinship with women and children, his prayerfulness, above all his love. Mr. C. F. Andrews has said that in Francis there is an illuminating parallel to Gandhi's "amazing sweetness and child-like innocence." "For I could easily imagine Gandhi preaching to the birds, embracing the leper, wearing the coarse dress of the half-naked poor, counting a rude beating in the snow by some churlish janitor as 'perfect joy.'

Whenever I read the *Little Flowers of St. Francis* with its mediæval setting, I say to myself, 'What a strange thing this is! Why, I have been witnessing this very life of love in Gandhi himself and in many of his followers also!'" Both Gandhi and Francis have occupied territories to which the other is a stranger. Gandhi does not share Francis's triumphant certainties nor his vast spiritual experience: Francis never had to put his teaching to so fiery a test, nor did he have the opportunity of applying it to the political life of Europe. But in this chapter the follower of Francis will see many points of resemblance between his patron and our Indian saint.

We shall first consider what is fundamental to Mahatma Gandhi—the life of poverty and the life of rule, and the three ultimate values of his philosophy, Truth, Purity, and Love. Then we will describe his teaching on such things as Sacrifice, Joy, Humility, Courage, Prayerfulness, and the reign of Religion over every part of life. We will discuss the quality of his nationalism, describe his own attitude and that of his followers to the poor, to the drink question, to hand-spinning and the emanicpation of women, and then conclude with an estimate (not our own, but borrowed from more competent authority) of his achievements.

III

Poverty

The first time I saw Mahatma Gandhi was at the beginning of 1928. It was then that Mr. C. F. Andrews delivered the Convocation Address at the Gujerat Vidyapeth, the National University at Ahmedabad, in the course of which occurred a passage which seemed to me to strike the keynote of the Mahatma's life. "India is a pilgrim of eternity," said Mr. Andrews, "who has set out on her search for the Eternal. She has laid aside the glory of the world and taken up the robe of the Sannyasi. Others who are satisfied with earthly riches may despise her in her poverty and her tattered robes. But the true children of India who can be satisfied with nothing but the Truth itself will revere even the tattered robe of their mother as she goes on her pilgrimage seeking not earthly riches but the vision of God Himself."

Everything in Gandhi's life is related to this idea. He is the citizen of a starving nation. His own standard of living, therefore, must correspond in some way to the average income of the people. "I am full of weaknesses and sins," he said to some friends. "But I have this one thing that the poor recognize in me at once: they know that I share all their hardships. You could have the same influence if you would do the same." And so Gandhi, the virtual Dictator of India, who could at a word, command the utmost luxury, lives as a poor peasant.

He has reduced his food to a minimum. He travels third class—a supreme asceticism in the crowded East. He accepts no gifts for himself. He will not exercise any rights over his writings. His clothing is the simplest possible and therefore of a remarkable beauty and dignity. You feel overdressed in the presence of this half-naked fakir. His room at the Sabarmati Ashram is furnished only with the bare necessities of life. The hut at Keradi (where he was arrested in 1930) was simply a poor peasant's hut, standing beneath the trees which encircled a little lake. It was a symbol of the new form of government, the rule of the poor, for the poor, by the poor. The prison-cell has no terrors for the Mahatma. On the occasion of his arrest in 1922, he was able to declare, "How should prison life and fare be a privation to me, since they could not possibly be simpler than the life and food I am accustomed to?"

The ever-present memory of the poor is thus the first motive for simplicity of life. "The test of orderliness in a country is not the number of millionaires it owns, but the absence of starvation among its masses." We have no right to more wealth than the average. If we would help the poor, we must live with them and live like them. Gandhi once asked the workers of Bardoli: "Have you a genuine love and sympathy for the dumb masses whose cause you are out to serve? Have you completely identified yourselves with them and their sufferings? Do you feel like taking up the broom and cleaning their latrines if they are dirty?" It is his ideal to approach the poor with the mind of the poor. When he was attacked by Communists in Bombay for betraying the cause of labour, he was able to reply, "I had made the working men's cause my own before any of the young Communists here were born. I spent the best part of my time in South Africa working for them. I used to live with them and shared their joys and sorrows."

A second motive is that, in Gandhi's view, it is the poor who live closest to nature and most in harmony with nature's laws. "It is theft if one receives anything which one does not really need. The fine truth at the bottom of this principle is that nature provides just enough and no more for our daily need." We must not therefore "possess unnecessary foodstuffs, clothing, or furniture." In observing this principle we are led to "a progressive simplification of our own lives."

Gandhi has rescued, out of the old ideal of total renunciation which could be practised only by the few, the new asceticism of simplicity which is open to all. The spiritual civilization of the future will be based on asceticism, which is simply another word for self-sacrifice or love. "Civilization in the real sense of the term consists not in the multiplication but in the deliberate and voluntary reduction of wants, which promotes real happiness and contentment, and increases the capacity for service."

The third motive for poverty is our sense of God. "A seeker after truth," Gandhi wrote last year from his prison-cell, "a follower of the Law of Love, cannot hold anything against to-morrow. . . . If we repose faith in God's providence, we should rest assured that He will give us every day our daily bread, supplying enough that we require."

From the *Bhagavadgita*, he learnt that he "could not follow God unless he gave up all that he had." He learnt the idea of trusteeship, "that those who desired salvation should act like the trustee, who, though having control over great possessions, regards not an iota of it as his own." He allowed his insurance policy to lapse, for he became convinced "that God who created his wife and children as well as himself would take care of them." He told his brother that henceforth all his savings would be utilized not for the benefit of his family, but for the good of the whole community.

A few incidents in the life of the Mahatma will vividly illustrate this ideal of Holy Poverty, and the strictness with which he interprets it. In his room at Sabarmati there was a piece of lattice-work which let the sun fall on his face, and since this troubled him he asked for it to be covered. Someone fetched a carpenter and suggested that a shutter might be erected. Gandhi agreed, but almost immediately realized this as an extravagance, and at the prayers that night confessed his fault. "Now this," he said, "is not what we who are pledged to poverty may do. It ought to have occurred to me that a piece of cardboard or a piece of cloth would serve as well as this shutter which costs a couple of rupees and three hours' labour for the carpenter. The cardboard or the piece of old cloth would have cost nothing and anyone could have fixed it there with a couple of nails. It is in these simple little things that our creed is tested. The Kingdom of Heaven is for those who are poor in spirit."

Here is another illuminating incident. One of the members of the Ashram, Chaganlal Joshi, was summoned to appear as a witness in a criminal case. The court was far distant, but no money was sent for the fare. As a member of the Ashram, Chaganlal had no money or time of his own. Gandhi considered that the Ashram money was all public money and could not be used for such a purpose. Chaganlal was thus in the exact position of a poor peasant who in similar circumstances would be absolutely helpless. So he decided to sit still and suffer the consequences. "Otherwise his voluntary poverty would have no meaning, nor could he serve the poor if he did not behave like them." Chaganlal was arrested for contempt of court, and taken before the magistrate, who, however, at once realized the mistake and released him. This incident illustrates the beauty and value of Poverty. Chaganlal was able to publish his experiences and reveal the fact that it was a common thing for peasants to be summoned for trials without being given their fares, a great hardship for poor men. Had he not behaved as if he were a poor peasant, this fact would not have been discovered.

In the course of Gandhi's march to Dandi, some of his followers incurred unnecessary expenses. Friends showered gifts upon the pilgrims. Gandhi was deeply moved. "We are marching," he said, "in the name of God. We profess to act on behalf of the hungry, the naked, the unemployed." For him to live above the means of the country would be like living on stolen food. He begged his hosts to be miserly rather than lavish. "This is not a battle to be conducted with money. . . . Extravagance has no room in this campaign. Success depends solely upon God. And He only helps the vigilant and the humble."

When Gandhi was in jail last year, he used to write many personal letters on tiny scraps of paper, and when asked his reason for this, he gave an answer which indicates much of his philosophy of Poverty. "Firstly," he said, "a prisoner must make use of the least possible quantity of things. Secondly, one who is under the vow of *Aparigraha* (non-possession) is the trustee and guardian of all property, and hence I must make use of the jail property like a miser. Thirdly, this property also belongs to us, does it not? With whose money is it acquired? Fourthly, we should make as little use as possible of such things in a country as poor as ours. Fifthly, under such circumstances my soul feels miserable if I make use of more things than necessary."

IV

Self-Control

The second time I saw Mahatma Gandhi was in Bombay, and then I was impressed not only with his poverty but with his supreme power of control, control of both mind and body.

It was at a great meeting of workers gathered in

the labour-area of Bombay. All around, the mills and gloomy tenements rose dark and sinister in the flaring light of the street-lamps. It was a Congress meeting, arranged to deepen Gandhi's fellowship with the mill-hands, but a party of Communists had captured the platform and had hoisted the Red Flag above it. High on the dais silhouetted against the sky sat the Mahatma; in front of him stood a mill-worker of magnificent physique, holding the Red Flag. With his splendid head and flashing eyes he looked the very symbol of Young Revolution. Two Communist orators rose one after the other and denounced the Mahatma for his supposed betrayal of the workers' cause. It was their intention to prevent him speaking, and they continued their abusive denunciation till everyone was exasperated. But Gandhi, with no trace of annoyance or impatience, took out his *takli* and began to spin with the utmost unconcern. When he was allowed to speak, he answered with perfect courtesy, in quiet and even tones, unperturbed by the hissing, shouting, and mocking laughter with which he was constantly interrupted. Here was one token of his amazing control of the mind.

The following morning I attended the prayers on the roof of his Bombay residence. It was four o'clock in the morning. Around and below us, the great city lay wrapped in slumber. Above, the stars shone clear and lovely. Here, on this quiet roof, sat the man of destiny, wrapped in a shawl, on a thin mattress spread on the cold stone, seeking from God the strength for his day's work. In the darkness, his white-clad form shone (so it seemed) with a strange mystic light. Two beautiful hymns were sung: there was a long reading from the Gita; there was a pause of silence, while all sat motionless in the contact of eternity. And then the day's labours leaped upon him. His secretary came forward with a pile of telegrams, and after a few minutes the President of the Congress arrived to take him for his morning walk.

Before I left I was told how Gandhi and his party had just travelled down from Delhi, a long thousand miles, third class; how at every station the crowd broke into the compartment to have his *darshan*; how they had had no rest that day and how Gandhi had not got to bed till 2.30 that very morning. And yet I found him an hour later, awake, fresh and strong, full of optimism and laughter. Not for anything would he miss his prayers. That was my next lesson, the unique control of the body by a dominant moral energy.

The truth is that Mahatma Gandhi has attained a state of equipoise which will keep him calm and unhurried under every circumstance. He has been quoted as saying that we must do our work with the energy and velocity of the Punjab Express, but never lose our balance and our capacity to free ourselves from it when necessary. "My impression about him," exclaims one of his disciples, "is that most of the things that hold men in bondage, things internal as well as external, no longer have their hold on him." He is able to sit unmoved under the rain of countless telegrams, endless visitors, the business of conducting three weeklies, the noise of crowds outside shouting for his *darshan*, perhaps even the hourly expectation of arrest. He never becomes "nervy" or disturbed.

The constancy of his discipline, which is the real source of his mind-control, is no less remarkable. This at first sight is so strict as to seem open to the charge of rigorism, until we remember that the Mahatma is realizing in his own life what is perhaps the greatest need of the National Movement. His own loyalty to rule must be super-eminent if it is to awaken a similar consistency in his followers. "The path of self-purification," he says, "is hard and steep. To attain to perfect purity a man has to rise above the opposing currents of love and hatred, attachment and repulsion, and to become absolutely passion-free in thought, speech, and action." How is this to be obtained save by humility which places "himself last among his fellow-creatures" and by a lifetime of disciplined aspiration? Let us simply note here Gandhi's unwavering allegiance to the spinning-wheel, his diet-experiments which aim at the complete control of the palate, his ideal and practice of *Brahmacharya* (chastity), his days of silence with which not even his release from prison can interfere. On returning from the Viceroy's house, after the attaining of the Delhi Pact, at 1.30 a.m. he did his daily quota of yarn, went to bed at 3.0 and was up for prayers at 4.0. He never misses his spinning or his prayer, whether he is engaged on a fast or in jail, or in the palaces of the wealthy.

His preaching on the subject of discipline has great significance for modern India.

Non-Co-operation (wrote Gandhi at the beginning of 1921) is not a movement of brag, bluster, or bluff. It is a test of our sincerity. It requires solid and silent self-sacrifice. It challenges our honesty and our capacity for national work. It is a movement which aims at translating ideas into action.

Discipline is the pledge and guarantee that a man means business. "There is no deliverance and no hope without sacrifice, discipline, and self-control. Mere sacrifice without discipline will be unavailing." It is very easy to shout war-cries, even when it is dangerous to do so; it is very hard to maintain, month after month, positive and constructive work for the nation. "The greatest task before the nation to-day," said Gandhi ten years ago, "is to discipline its demonstrations if they are to serve any useful purpose." It is just this discipline which is itself the most effective demonstration. "The moment we show intelligent organization, honest but unbendable purpose, and perfect and disciplined cohesion, the English will hand over the whole administration to us without a blow."

The truest freedom is bondage to a higher law. "A man who chooses the path of freedom from restraint," Gandhi told a schoolboys' conference at Ahmedabad, "will be a bond-slave of passions, whilst the man who binds himself to rules and restraints releases himself. All things in the universe, including the sun and the moon and the stars, obey certain laws, and without the restraining influence of those laws the world would not go on for a single moment. You, whose mission in life is service of your fellow-men, will go to pieces if you do not impose on yourself some sort of discipline, and prayer is a necessary spiritual discipline. It is discipline and restraint that separates us from the brute. If we will be men walking with our heads erect and not walking on all fours, let us understand and put ourselves under voluntary discipline and restraint."

Gandhi has drawn a very attractive picture of the true Congressman, disciplined, brave and pure, by no means uncommon among his followers.

> A true Congressman is a true servant. He ever gives, ever wants to serve. He is easily satisfied so long as his own comfort is concerned. He is always content to take a back seat. He is never communal or provincial. His country is his paramount consideration. He is brave to a fault because he has shed all earthly ambitions, fear of Death itself. And he is generous because he is brave, forgiving because he is humble and conscious of his own failing and limitations.

There can be no doubt that the ideal of discipline has spread widely during the last ten years. Despite occasional outbreaks of mob-violence and rioting, the mass of the people has remained peaceful and restrained even in times of great excitement or of acute provocation. The "Satyagraha Army" has, as we should expect, especially developed in this respect. Mr. Natarajan, Editor of the *Indian Social Reformer*, wrote in June 1930, "In 1921 one heard now and then of 'White Caps' (that is, people wearing the Gandhi caps), in an inebriated condition, shouting 'Mahatma ki jai.' No one hears of such things now. They have become a disciplined army without arms, prepared to suffer but not to inflict suffering—gentle, helpful, tolerant, and incorruptible. Not long ago I was talking to a high Baroda official. The talk drifted to the flood relief three years ago, and he spoke of the service of the 'White Caps,' with warm admiration. 'Not a pie,' he said, 'was misapplied by them.' "

On his great march to Dandi, Mahatma Gandhi

insisted on the strictest discipline. In spite of all weariness and difficulty, the routine had to be followed. Every volunteer had to attend the prayers, do his allotted spinning, and write up his daily diary. "Ours is a sacred pilgrimage, and self-examination and self-purification are essentials which we cannot do without." Their Satyagraha was a sacrificial offering, and must be pure. Soul-force can only be generated by a rigorous self-discipline. On entering the districts in which Civil Disobedience was to be offered, Gandhi urged his followers to greater purification and intenser dedication. They were not to allow themselves to be pampered. There must be no luxuries. Expenses must be kept at the minimum.

Rabindranath Tagore, in his own fashion, gave the same message to the country.

"The sacrifice needed for serving our country," said the Poet to the boys and girls of the Sabarmati Ashram on his last visit at the beginning of 1930, "must not consist in merely emotional enthusiasm which is indulged in as a sort of luxury, but it should be a real discipline of truth. . . . Let us not talk, but have faith in silent work, faith in humble beginnings, and I know Truth will take wing of itself and like fire will spread through the country, though its origin may be small and insignificant."

V

Let us now consider some aspects of the spiritual teaching of Mahatma Gandhi The three ruling principles, the ultimate values in his life, are Truth, Purity, and Love. The fact that he often uses Sanskrit names for these values, and often in speaking of the third calls it by the negative term, "non-violence" or *Ahimsa*, must not blind Western readers to the close kinship which in this respect at least he bears to their own thought.

TRUTH

For Mahatma Gandhi, the ideal of Truth is rooted in his vision of God. "The word '*Satya*' (Truth) is derived from *Sat*,[1] meaning 'to be.' *Satya* then is being. Nothing but Truth has existence. Hence the definition of God is *Sat*. Better that Truth should be called God, than God Truth." "For me," he says again, "Truth is the sovereign principle which includes numerous other principles. This Truth is not only truthfulness in word, but truthfulness in thought also, and not only the relative truth of our conception, but the Absolute Truth, the Eternal Principle, that is, God . . . I worship God as Truth only. I have not yet found Him, but I am seeking after Him. I am prepared to sacrifice the things dearest to me in pursuit of this quest. Even if the sacrifice demanded be my very life, I hope I may be prepared to give it. . . . Often in my progress I have had faint glimpses of the Absolute Truth, God, and daily conviction is growing upon me that He alone is real and all else is unreal."

[1] *Sat* is the neuter singular of the present participle of the Sanskrit verb "to be," and thus answers exactly to the Greek.

When Gandhi resumed his task of editing *Young India* in 1924, he set the tone of the paper in his declaration: "I want to see God face to face. God, I *know*, is Truth. For me the only certain means of knowing God is non-violence—*Ahimsa*—Love. I live for India's freedom and would die for it, because it is a part of Truth. Only a free India can worship the true God."

In this last quotation we get a hint of the great principle that Truth contains in itself all other moral values. For this reason, Truth is placed first among the "Observances" of the Ashram at Sabarmati. "Truth is God, the One and only Reality. All other observances take their rise from the quest for, and the worship of, Truth." Truth is the basis, as well as the goal of knowledge. "Where there is Truth, there is knowledge—pure and simple. Where Truth is not pure, knowledge cannot exist."

Truth is intimately connected with self-control. "All our principles," wrote Gandhi from his prison-cell, "arise out of the main one—Truth. How can one who is attempting to realize Truth worship sensual passion? We know of no one who has realized Truth by leading a sensual life."

Truth is a loyal ally of non-violence, the constant friend of love. "Search after Truth without non-violence is impossible. Non-violence and Truth are inseparable like the two sides of a coin. Non-violence is the means and Truth the aim. Truth is God and there is only one way to realize Him and that is the path of non-violence."

Gandhi's conception of the relation of Truth and

Art is of great interest. "Truth is the first thing to be sought for, and Beauty and Goodness will then be added to you. That is what Christ really taught in the Sermon on the Mount. Jesus was to my mind a supreme Artist because He saw and expressed Truth: and so was Mohammed. Scholars say that the Koran is the most perfect composition in all Arabic literature. Because both of them strove first for Truth, therefore the grace of expression naturally came in. Yet neither Jesus nor Mohammed wrote on art. That is the Truth and Beauty I crave for, live for and would die for." Elsewhere he has said that he did not find Truth through Beauty, but Beauty through Truth. "All truths, not merely true ideas, but truthful faces, truthful pictures, truthful songs, are highly beautiful. Whenever men begin to see Beauty in Truth, then art will arise."

If we are ever to find the Absolute Truth, which is God, we must be faithful in every detail to what Gandhi calls "relative Truth"; that is to say all those little unremembered duties of honesty and faithfulness which daily confront us in our ordinary life. "As long as I have not realized the Absolute Truth, so long must I hold by the relative Truth as I have conceived it. That relative Truth must meanwhile be my beacon, my shield, and buckler Though this path is straight and narrow as a razor's edge, for me it has been the quickest and easiest." The votary of Truth will scrupulously avoid all forms of exaggeration or manipulation of facts. He will conceal neither the faults of his friends nor the virtues of his enemies. He will be no party to subterfuge or concealment. His promise will be "inflexible and unbreakable." It will give him courage.

Along this pathway of relative Truth, the pilgrim soul will come one day to the perfect and ultimate reality, the beatific vision of God, the Absolute Truth.

VI

Purity

The name by which the Purity of the soul and control of all the senses is known in India is *Brahmacharya*—a word which is constantly to be found in the Mahatma's writings.

"*Brahmacharya* properly and fully understood means search after Brahma." This is the same as self-conquest and realization. "Realization is impossible without complete control of all the senses. Therefore *Brahmacharya* signifies control of all the senses at all times and at all places in thought, word, and deed." Its most obvious application is, of course, to sexual morality, but its actual reference is far wider. "Only he who struggles hard against the allurements of sense-objects and turns in tears and grief to the Lord will be comforted." So Gandhi teaches that those who would aim at inner purity must live a life of all-round discipline. The sense of taste must be controlled. We must take food as we would medicine. We must control our eyes. It is good to walk with eyes cast down so that they may not wander away to alluring objects. We must not wear overmuch clothing. Conversation and company must be adjusted. The ideal way of *Brahmacharya* is, however, by sublimation and by prayer. "The whole world will be to him one vast family. . . . He will centre all his ambitions in relieving the misery of mankind. He who has realized the misery of mankind in all its magnitude will never be stirred by passion. He will instinctively know the fountain of strength in him, and he will ever persevere to keep it undefiled." He will best gain this strength by prayer. "A heartfelt prayer every day for purity makes one progressively pure." Prayer "becomes one's staff of life and carries one through every ordeal."

We do not intend to discuss here Gandhi's view of Celibacy, his own vow of abstinence from sexual relationships and his desire to see it imitated. We are concerned rather with his inner spiritual ideal of purity. A beautiful illustration of this will be found in the story of the marriage of his son, Ramdas. Gandhi would not consent to the marriage till the bride had finished her seventeenth year. Ramdas was thirty. The engagement lasted two years. The keynote of the marriage ceremony was a solemn simplicity. Before it began, bride and bridegroom were asked to consecrate it by fasting, manual labour in the shape of spinning and cleaning the well-basin, cleaning the cowshed, watering the trees so as to symbolize unity with the whole creation, and reading a chapter from the *Bhagavadgita*. The ceremony was very simple, a vow of faithfulness and dedication to service made before the Sacrificial Fire. There was no music and nothing like a wedding-party or dinner. The wedding presents were few and simple, and symbolized service. Bride and bridegroom were both dressed in white Khadi, without any gold or other ornaments. Gandhi, who was deeply moved by the event, said in the course of his speech, "You will guard your wife's honour and be not her master, but her true friend. You will hold her body and her soul as sacred as I trust she will hold your body and your soul. To that end you will have to live a life of prayerful toil, and simplicity and self-restraint. . . . Let your lives be consecrated to the service of the Motherland, and toil away until you wear out your bodies."

VII

Love

The third ideal fundamental to Gandhi's mind is *Ahimsa*, Non-violence, Love. Gandhi has himself expressly identified the three terms. "The true rendering of the word *Ahimsa* in English is Love, or Charity." "In its positive form, Ahimsa means the largest love, the greatest charity." "For me the only certain means of knowing God is non-violence, *Ahimsa*, Love." This spirit of love radiates from the great heart of the Mahatma. No one need be a stranger to his friendliness. He is the most accessible of men. His love is unconquerable. It is infectious. It breaks down every barrier. It lives among his followers. I myself have seen the power of his love shining within the grim walls of the prison, beneath the canvas roofs of the emigrant camp, in the bandaged faces of the lathi-shattered victims in the hospitals. He is indeed great who can bear such love in his own heart, but what shall we say of him who can reproduce it in a thousand lives?

Love is a supreme ally even of the politician. "Love is the strongest force the world possesses, and yet it is the humblest imaginable." No one has more reason to hate than Gandhi, for no one in the world has gazed more often on the open face of injustice and oppression than he, and yet he can say, "I hold myself to be incapable of hating any being on earth. By a long course of prayerful discipline I have ceased for over forty years to hate anybody." "Mine is not an exclusive love. I cannot love Mussulmans or Hindus and hate Englishmen; for, if I merely love Hindus and Mussulmans because their ways are on the whole pleasing to me, I shall soon begin to hate them when their ways displease me, as they may well do any moment. A love that is based on the goodness of those you love is a mercenary affair, whereas true love is self-effacing and demands no consideration."

Love in fact will never be content with local or provincial boundaries; it will ever strive to open arms of greeting to the whole world. Love redeems mere nationalism with a vision of world-wide generosity. "My goal is friendship with the world." "Having flung aside the sword," he said recently, "there is nothing except the cup of love which I can offer to those who oppose me. It is by offering that cup that I expect to draw them close to me. I cannot think of permanent enmity between man and man, and believing as I do in the theory of rebirth, I live in the hope that if not in this birth, in some other birth I shall be able to hug all humanity in friendly embrace." Love is nothing less than the humble service of humanity. "I must prove to everyone that I am what I profess to be—their friend and servant. My creed is service of God and therefore of humanity. . . . Voluntary service means pure love. I must strive my utmost to express in every little act of mine whatever love I am capable of." "Love so deep-seated as it is in me will not be sacrificed even for the realm of the whole world."

Love in the active, public political sphere is named non-violence. This is not, as its name might imply, a merely negative quality. "This talk of passive non-resistance," said Gandhi one night at the Ashram, "has been the bane of our national life. Forgiveness is a quality of the soul, and therefore a positive quality. It is not negative. 'Conquer anger,' says Lord Buddha, 'by non-anger.' But what is that 'non-anger'? It is a positive quality and means the supreme virtue of charity or love."

"This Non-violence," says Mahatma Gandhi, "is the first article of my faith. It is also the last article of my creed." The exact words are of vital importance, for it must never be forgotten that the Mahatma's non-violence is not a mere policy; it is a creed. "My love for non-violence is superior to every other thing, mundane or super-mundane. It is equalled only by my love for Truth, which to me is synonymous with non-violence, through which alone I can see and reach Truth." Non-violence is grounded in the dignity of human nature. "Non-violence is the law of our species as violence is the law of the brute. The spirit lies dormant in the brute and he knows no law but that of physical might. The dignity of man requires obedience to a higher law—to the strength of the spirit."

What is the true meaning of non-violence? It is not mere restraint from physical violence. It is an affair of the whole personality. "Evil thoughts, rashness, ill-will, hatred, and falsehoods are all forms of violence. To possess what others need is also violence. If I harbour ill-will in my breast, but do not express it in acts, I am still violent. By non-violence, or peace, I mean the peace which comes through inner strength. If I have that peace, I won't have any hate in me."

Non-violence is the natural creed of India, the home of religion, of toleration, of gentleness. It is woven into the fabric of her national idealism. "India cannot win her freedom by violence for a century, because her people are not built in the manner of other nations. They have been nurtured in the traditions of suffering." "Violence is for us a gospel of despair." "Let not your rock be violence and devilry. Our rock must be non-violence and godliness." Violence is ineffective, unnatural, the origin of untold evils. "Any violence on our part must be a token of our stupidity, ignorance, and impotent rage." "Armed risings are a remedy worse than the disease sought to be cured. They are a token of the spirit of revenge and impatience and anger. The message of violence cannot do good in the long run."

On the other hand "what is obtained by love is retained for all time. What is obtained by hatred proves a burden in reality; for it increases hatred." "Satyagraha—the Law of Love—is the law of life. Departure from it leads to disintegration. A firm adherence to it leads to regeneration." Gandhi draws on the lives of saints and yogis to show that truly gentle souls will never be hurt by wild animals. "The great St. Francis of Assisi, who used to roam about the forests, was not hurt by the serpents or the wild beasts, nay, they even lived on terms of intimacy with him." This principle will apply both to our relations with the animals and with our human enemies. "I have implicit faith in the doctrine that so long as man is not inimical to the other creatures, they will not be inimical to him. Love is the greatest of the attributes of man. Without it the worship of God would be an empty nothing. It is, in short, the root of all religions whatsoever."

Truly "love never faileth." Such is the Mahatma's message to the world. Let us cling to love with all our power. The real danger to the Satyagrahi is not prison, or the lathi, or scorn, or repression, but simply a little hatred that will deprive him of his power. "If India adopted the doctrine of love as an active part of her religion and introduced it in her politics, Swaraj would descend upon her as from heaven."

VIII

These fundamental ideals lead on the soul to others, some of which we will now consider. First, we will think of the Mahatma's teaching on sacrifice and his life of renunciation which sanctions it. Then we will notice the joy without which sacrifice is of no avail, and the humility and courage which enables the soul to leave all for the vision of the Truth. The Mahatma's life is essentially one of prayerful religious aspiration, and we shall see how it is that religion can be the inspiration and the guide of his political life.

Sacrifice

"His whole life," once said Tagore in speaking of the Mahatma, "is only another name for sacrifice." Sacrifice is the loveliest as well as the noblest of the possessions of mankind: it was created at the beginning of all things: it is the very principle of life. "Mankind," says Gandhi, "lives by sacrifice." *Yajna* (sacrifice) literally means worship, hence sacrifice, hence any sacrificial act or any act of service. Since sacrifice is the root of life and freedom is life lived on its most intense and perfect level, it follows that there can be no freedom without sacrifice. "The Temple of Freedom is not erected without the blood of sufferers," though this suffering is not to be the ordinary fruit of violent revolution. It is the way of non-violent suffering that alone can lead direct to freedom. For suffering purifies the soul, and only the pure soul is free. Swaraj gained without suffering might mean only a new kind of servitude, for self-government is not synonymous with freedom. "No country in the world has gained its liberty, has seen a new birth without difficulty, without pain, without sacrifice. And what is sacrifice? The right meaning of sacrifice that I learnt in my youth was that it meant making sacred, making holy. Non-Co-operation is a process of purification."

The Mahatma gives an altogether new meaning to the ancient ideal of Renunciation in the East. It "does not mean abandoning the world and retiring into the forest, but the infusion of the spirit of renunciation into all the activities of life." The householder, the merchant, the tailor, the barber, the weaver, may all live the dedicated life. When they think of the welfare of others, their life becomes artistic in the real sense of the term. "A life of sacrifice is the pinnacle of Art, and is full of true relish[1] which ever renews itself. A man is never surfeited with it, and the spring of interest is ever inexhaustible. . . . Indulgence leads to destruction and renunciation to immortality." Renunciation is not social death but social service. "Sacrifice means service," it means "laying down one's life so that others may live." "Let us suffer, so that others may be happy; the highest service and the highest love is that wherein man lays down his life for his fellow-men."

[1] *Rasa* (relish), according to Hindu æsthetics, is the essence of poetry.

IX

Joy

Mahatma Gandhi possesses to the fullest degree that hall-mark of saintliness—the spirit of joy. He is a man capable of great sorrows, and the burden of his nation's tragedy often presses upon his heart: but his optimism is unconquerable and his smile the most characteristic thing about him. Mrs. Naidu has spoken of "that happy laugh of his that seems to hold all the undimmed radiance of the world's childhood in its depths." He has a fund of good humour and kindliness. There is a sort of radiant courtesy about him, which never flags even when he is distracted by a thousand worries. This man of vast renunciations finds in sacrifice the fullness of joy. "Suffering cheerfully endured ceases to be suffering and is transmuted into an ineffable joy."

It is in his love of children that the spirit of joy finds its most natural expression. When he is free he is always surrounded by them; when he is imprisoned they are constantly in his thoughts. During my last visit to Sabarmati, the Mahatma's letters which had just arrived from the jail were read aloud at the evening prayers. It was a beautiful and touching sight to see the children gathering round the reader, their faces alive with eagerness and excitement. One such letter from jail, one of the most charming children's letters ever written, has become famous.

LITTLE BIRDS,

Ordinary birds cannot fly without wings. With wings, of course, all can fly. But if you, without wings, will learn how to fly, then all your troubles will indeed be at an end. And I will teach you.

See, I have no wings, yet I come flying to you every day in thought. Look, here is little Vimala, here is Hari, and here Dharmakumar. And you also can come flying to me in thought.

There is no need for a teacher for those who know how to think. The teacher may guide us, but he cannot give us the power of thinking. That is latent in us. Those who are wise get wise thoughts.

Tell me who, amongst you, are not praying properly in Prabhubhai's evening prayer.

Send me a letter signed by all and those who do not know how to sign may make a cross.

Bapu's blessings

YERAWDA PALACE,
Silence Day

X

HUMILITY

Both in his life and teaching, Gandhi lays great stress on Humility. It is the secret of his power. His enemies feel that in him they are opposing a man who is seeking nothing for himself, either of money, prestige, or fame. He is eager for opposition and criticism. He shrinks from praise, but abuse never disturbs him. "I have learnt from the New Testament, as also from other sources, that, if one wishes to walk in the fear of God, one should be indifferent about popular praise or blame." He has not set himself up on a throne of moral superiority; if any of his followers do wrong, he seeks the cause of it in his own heart. If there is anyone generally despised or condemned, he will seek him out to help him by his company. So far is he from desiring to dominate others that he lives in his own Ashram as though he were a guest. He is always ready to admit mistakes, just as he has confessed his past failures and the long pathway which he feels he has yet to tread. "I must reduce myself to zero. So long as one does not of his own free will put himself last among his fellow-creatures, there is no salvation for him. *Ahimsa* is the farthest limit of humility."

"The spirit of non-violence," he says, "necessarily leads to humility. Non-violence means reliance on God, the Rock of Ages," "We must act even as the mango-tree which droops as it bears fruit. Its grandeur lies in its majestic lowliness." Humility is the meek sister of non-violence, for humility is always reverent, quiet, restrained and loving.

Gandhi sees clearly that "humility never came to anyone by practice." "A humble person is not himself conscious of his humility." He simply sees himself in his right proportions. Such a vision "spells the utter destruction of egoism." We are only atoms in the great system of the universe. "But if we shatter the chains of egoism and reduce ourselves to nothingness, we shall become all in all. To feel that we are something is to set up a barrier between God and ourselves. To cease thinking that we are something is to become one with God."

The most original and beautiful part of Gandhi's

teaching on Humility is his stress on the relation between Humility and Service, between Humility and the true activity of the soul. "One who would sacrifice his life for others has hardly time to reserve for himself a place in the sun. Inertia must not be mistaken for humility as it has been in Hinduism. True humility means most strenuous and constant endeavour, entirely directed to the service of humanity. God is constantly performing action without resting for a single moment. If we would serve Him or become one with Him, our activity must be as unwearied as His. There may be rest in store for the drop which is separated from the ocean, but not for the drop in the ocean which knows no rest. The same is the case with ourselves. As soon as we become one with the ocean in the shape of God, there is no more rest for us, nor indeed do we need rest any longer. This restlessness constitutes true rest. This never-ceasing agitation holds the key to peace ineffable. True humility therefore demands the sacrifice of everything that we have at the altar of humility."

XI

Courage

In no respect is the influence of Mahatma Gandhi more strikingly illustrated than in the new mentality of courageous self-respect which he has infused into the nation. Courage is the one sure foundation of character. Without courage there is no morality, no religion, no love. "One cannot follow truth or love," says Gandhi, "so long as one is subject to fear." "Where there is fear there is no religion." Fearlessness is a *sine qua non* for the growth of the other noble qualities. "Cowardice is a thing even more hateful than violence, simply because cowardice usually results in violence." Gandhi himself relates how "as a coward, which I was for years, I harboured violence; I began to prize non-violence only when I began to shed cowardice."

For India to-day, courage is a primary need. As there is a reign of fear in the country, meditation on and cultivation of fearlessness have a particular importance. "A seeker after Truth must give up the fear of parents, caste, Government, robbers, etc., and he must not be frightened by poverty or death." "Before we can aspire to guide the destinies of India we shall have to adopt this habit of fearlessness."

What then is this courage and how is it obtained? There are two kinds of courage. One is "the momentary excitement that blinds people and makes them create a splash for a moment. That kind of excitement cannot bring Swaraj. I can conceive its use for a fighting people prepared to wrest power from other hands." But the 'excitement' of the Satyagrahi is not like that. "It dies in such an atmosphere. It needs the development of calm courage that knows no defeat and despises revenge." The really courageous Satyagrahi will be "patient, absolutely truthful, absolutely non-violent, yes in thought, word and deed, and gentle towards his opponents." This courage in fact is a reasoned and deliberate abandonment of every kind of external fear—"fear of disease, bodily injury and death, of dispossession, of losing one's nearest and dearest, of losing reputation, or giving offence and so on." It is a moral virtue. "Bravery on the battlefield is impossible for us. Bravery of the soul still remains open to us. I am engaged in evoking that bravery. Non-Co-operation means nothing less than training in self-sacrifice." Courage in fact is the sacrificial attitude towards life, it is unfettered selflessness, it is love in action.

Courage is gained first of all by a true fear. "There is only One whom we have to fear, that is God. When we fear God, then we shall fear no man, however high-placed he may be; and if you want to follow the vow of Truth, then fearlessness is absolutely necessary."

The second condition, as Gandhi reminded the country in one of his letters from prison, is detachment. "All fears revolve round the body as the centre, and will therefore disappear as soon as we get rid of the attachment for the body. We thus find that all fear is the baseless fabric of our own vision." When we have shaken off all attachment for wealth, for family, and for the body, regarding these things "not as proprietors, but as only trustees," realizing that "nothing whatever in this world is ours, even we ourselves are His," we shall cast off our craven fears. Pride is thus in a sense the cause of fear, and it is as we become humble that we become courageous. "When we cease to be masters and reduce ourselves to the rank of servants, humbler than the very dust under our feet, all fears will roll away like mists; we shall attain ineffable peace, and see *Satyanarayan* (the God of Truth) face to face."

But in the last resort, only Love can conquer fear. "Perfect love casteth out fear." In the words of the hymn by Pritamdas, so often sung to Gandhi during the great Fast of 1924:

> The pathway of love is the ordeal of fire. The shrinker turns away from it. . . .
> Love is a priceless thing, only to be won at the cost of death.
> Those who live to die, these attain, for they have shed all thoughts of self.
> Those heroic souls who are rapt in the love of the Lord, they are the true lovers.

Death itself, as this hymn clearly shows, must be met and conquered. "Swaraj is the abandonment of the fear of death. A nation which allows itself to be influenced by the fear of death cannot attain Swaraj, and cannot retain it if somehow attained." "We are not yet completely free because we are not prepared to look death quietly in the face." Perhaps, after all, death is the least terrifying of life's reversals. "Death at any time is blessed," wrote Gandhi on the death of Swami Shraddhananda, "but it is twice blessed for a warrior who dies for his cause, i.e. Truth. Death is no fiend, he is the truest of friends. He delivers us from agony. He helps us against ourselves. He even gives us new chances, new hopes. He is like sleep, a sweet restorer."

This teaching came with a breath of exhilaration and power to India. Both by example and precept Gandhi taught that the only way of freedom was fearlessness. There can be no fear in Satyagraha for Satyagraha is love, and perfect love casteth out fear. It was a wonderful experience to watch a whole nation throwing off its mental bonds of servitude, and rising to its true dignity of fearless determination.

"The national upheaval," wrote Jairamdas Daulatram in June 1930, "has well-nigh broken the mental bonds of slavery. Man, woman, and child are learning to hold their heads high and breathe as free beings. The dread of imprisonment is gone. The fear of bullets and lathis is also going. The rich and the poor are developing their capacity for sacrifice. Above the echoes of past inter-communal discord, a new symphony of national unification is becoming audible."

This courage was illustrated by those who faced the lathi with quiet heroism at Dharasana or on the Azad Maidan. It is said that the courage of the people has grown since 1921. Many more are ready to die for their ideal. To-day the story of the volunteers in Bihar, the sacrifice of the Volunteer Hiralal at Benares, the quiet endurance of thousands in the jails, the readiness for sacrifice shown by the peasants of Gujerat, has opened a new page in India's history.

It needs a tremendous courage not to strike back. It needs great courage to go to jail naturally and cheerfully. I was talking one day last December to Mr. Ramdas Gandhi (the Mahatma's third son) when the police came to arrest him. I shall never forget how he went away: there was no fuss, no display, but just courtesy and good cheer: he went to his cell with the courage and bearing of a prince.

Mr. C. F. Andrews stresses this changed mentality in his *India and the Simon Report.* He was talking one day to an Indian friend who was bitterly condemning the whole Non-Co-operation Movement for its futility. When he had finished his tirade, Mr. Andrews put to him a simple question:

"Does the Indian villager to-day," he asked, "stand up to the Englishman more fearlessly than before? Has he become less afraid of the Government official, of the landowner, and of the police?"

The friend paused suddenly, as if a new thought had struck him for the first time.

"You're right," he said, "I never thought of that. Of course there's no comparison. The villager looks every man in the face to-day."

XII

Spirituality

For Mahatma Gandhi, the spiritual is the supremely real. It is by spiritual values that he estimates the worth of all his actions; he is never forgetful of the spiritual world which is the true home of his great soul.

"With my hand on my breast I can say that not a minute in my life am I forgetful of God. For over twenty years I have been doing everything that I have done as in the presence of God." He claims that he is guided by the Spirit of God. "I do not claim to know definitely that all conscious thought and action on my part is directed by the Spirit. But on an examination of the greatest steps that I have taken in my life, as also of those that may be regarded as the least, I think that it will not be improper to say that all of them were directed by the Spirit." This is a tremendous claim, but it is made in deep humility.

Gandhi insists on a religious basis for all his movements and institutions. "No man," he says, "can live without religion. There are some who in the egotism of their reason declare that they have nothing to do with religion. But that is like a man saying that he breathes, but that he has no nose." Gandhi's religion is the pure and lofty dedication of the spirit of man to Truth. Only that man can be called religious whose mind is free from the taint of hatred or selfishness, and who leads a life of absolute purity and of disinterested service. Religion is "that which changes one's very nature, which binds one indissolubly to the Truth within, and which ever purifies. It is the permanent element in human nature which counts no cost too great in order to find full expression and which leaves the soul utterly restless until it has found itself, known its Maker, and appreciated the true correspondence between the Maker and itself."

Religion is essentially practical: it embraces the whole of life. This is especially true of the relations between religion and politics, a realm in which Gandhi has made one of his most important contributions to Eastern thought. "Politics divorced from religion has absolutely no meaning." "Economics to be worth anything must be capable of being reduced to terms of religion and spirituality." "My devotion to Truth has drawn me into the field of politics; and I can say without the slightest hesitation, and yet in all humility, that those who say that religion has nothing to do with politics do not know what religion means."

XIII

Prayer

The spiritual attitude to life is fed and strengthened by prayer. "I believe," says Gandhi, "that prayer is the very soul and essence of religion, and therefore prayer must be the very core of the life of man, for no man can live without religion." It was several days' continued prayer that led Gandhi to undertake his great Fast. Gently reproving those who once were impatient with his patience he pointed out that the most effective work may be unseen. "For years together in South Africa my efforts consisted practically only in waiting and prayer, and it is my firm conviction that that period of silent prayer was the most fruitful for that work. It constituted the bedrock on which whatever little was accomplished was based." It is prayer which is the condition of the search for Truth. "One discovers truth by patient endeavour and silent prayer. . . . Humble and constant endeavour and silent prayer are always my two trusty companions along the weary but beautiful path that all seekers must tread." It is prayer which purifies the heart. It is prayer which dignifies even the humblest duty. "A scavenger who works in God's service shares equal distinction with a king who uses his gifts in His name and as a mere trustee." It is prayer which elevates politics on to the ideal plane, for a good man's politics will be guided, coloured, and ennobled by his prayer."

What is prayer? "It is not an asking. It is a longing of the soul. It is a daily admission of one's weakness." It is "a yearning of the heart to be one with its Maker, an invocation for His blessing." "Prayer is a result of the realization of our helplessness and our final reliance upon God to the exclusion of all else." The Rule of the Sabarmati Ashram, speaking of the morning and evening worship, says, "it has been conceived as an aid to self-purification and dedication of one's all to God." Prayer may be both private and individual as well as corporate and congregational. "A congregational prayer is a mighty thing. What we do not often do alone, we do together. . . . It is a common experience for men who have no robust faith to seek the comfort of congregational prayer. All who flock to churches, temples, or mosques are not scoffers or humbugs. They are honest men and women. For them congregational prayer is like the daily bath, a necessity of their existence. These places of worship are not a mere idle superstition to be swept away at the first opportunity. They have survived all attacks up to now and are likely to persist to the end of time." "I feel very lonely," he once exclaimed, "without a congregation to share the prayer with me."

Since prayer is essentially a practical matter, it is good to set aside definite times when we will pray and to have fixed forms of prayer though we will not be bound by these. We are not to discard them because in the hands of the careless they have become mechanical and formal. We must ourselves rather see to it that we attain "the correct attitude to accompany these devotions." "Begin your day with prayer and make it so soulful that it may remain with you until the evening. Close the day with prayer so that you may have a peaceful night." There is a value in set forms due to the power of words. "Words after all acquire a power by long usage and sacredness associated with their use." On the other hand we must not be burdened by the form. "Let it be any form: it should be such as can put us into communion with the divine."

What are the conditions of prayer? "My religion says that only he who is prepared to suffer can pray to God." There must also be the penitential note about it. "Prayer is a confession of one's unworthiness and weakness. Prayer is not to be performed with the lips but with the heart. He, therefore, who would pray to God must cleanse his heart." It must be sincere. "I assure you that mere utterance parrot-wise of the name of God is of no avail." "It is better in prayer to have a heart without words than words without heart. It must be in clear response to the spirit which hungers for it. And even as a hungry man relishes a hearty meal, a hungry soul will relish a heart-felt prayer." Another condition of prayer is service. The Ashram prayers, it has been observed, strike a double note —the doing of selfless work and the freeing of the soul by such work from the bondage of matter. They emphasize the "high spiritual value of purified work as laying the very foundations of a truly religious life." "God of Himself seeks for His seat the heart of him who serves his fellow-men." "He who would be a *bhakta* must serve the suppressed and poverty-stricken by body, soul and mind." "Service makes the heart prayerful." Spinning on behalf of the poor is "the greatest prayer, the greatest worship, the greatest sacrifice."

It is impossible to estimate the effects of prayer. It brings "the purifying presence of God within the soul." It gives us the right attitude to life. "Nothing can be grander than to ask God to make us act justly towards everything that lives." It is the source of order. "Prayer is the only means of bringing about orderliness and peace and repose in our daily acts." "Without prayer there is no inward peace." Prayer frees the soul "from the layers of ignorance and darkness that envelop it. He, therefore, who hungers for the awakening of the divine in him must fall back on prayer."

XIV

Nationalism and Internationalism

What is the quality of Mahatma Gandhi's Nationalism? We must remember that it is primarily a moral rather than a political ideal. The Mahatma is hungry for freedom, as a man hungers for bread, because he knows that it is through freedom that he can bring bread to the hungry. He places Nationalism first because until India is a free nation she has no gift for the world. "India must learn to live before she can aspire to die for humanity." "An India prostrate at the feet of Europe can give no hope to humanity. An India awakened and free has a message of peace and good will to give to a groaning world." Nationalism is for India the annunciation of the fullness of life. "The rise of a National spirit in India," says Sir Francis Younghusband, "is a beautiful and splendid thing—a thing to be encouraged—the one and only thing that can make India and make her free and noble."

There is nothing narrow or provincial about the nationalism of Mahatma Gandhi and his followers. "My goal," declares the Mahatma, "is friendship with the world." "We shall live for the world-brotherhood and die for world-brotherhood. . . . The family love which comes in conflict with world-brotherhood is nothing worth." Jawaharlal Nehru, the young romantic leader, son of a noble house, who has been five times in jail, said at the National Congress at Christmas 1929, of which he was President:

Independence is not a happy word in the world to-day, for it means exclusiveness and isolation. Civilization has had enough of narrow nationalism, and gropes towards a wider co-operation and interdependence. And if we use the word independence, we do so in no sense hostile to the larger ideal. Independence for us means complete freedom from British domination and the British Imperialism. Having attained our freedom, I have no doubt that India will welcome all attempts at world co-operation and federation, and will even agree to give up part of her independence to a larger group of which she is an equal member.

Gandhi has the great ideal that India may help "to move the world and help weaker races." "My ambition is much higher than independence. Through the deliverance of India, I seek to deliver the so-called weaker races of the earth from the crushing heels of Western exploitation."

It is not against Britain that India is fighting. "It is not England that is our enemy," says Pandit Jawaharlal, "it is Imperialism." "The fight is not between the Indians and the English. It is between Imperialism and Socialism." India is warring against the pride of great nations; against force organized to destruction; against the haughty domination of the machine; against capitalist exploitation; for the right of self-determination for the weaker races; for the right of man to follow the Inner Voice wherever it may lead. Mahatma Gandhi was not imprisoned by the British; he was imprisoned by a false standard of values. As has been said, "Gandhi in jail is one philosophy of life awaiting crucifixion at the hands of another."

Mahatma Gandhi's own attitude to the British

is well known. It is shared by the majority of his followers. He deliberately chose to send his famous 1930 letter to the Viceroy by the hand of an Englishman, because he wanted a check on himself against any intentional act that would hurt a single Englishman. He has often acknowledged his debt to England. "No one will accuse me," said Gandhi on the eve of the last great struggle, "of any anti-English tendency. I have thankfully copied many things from them. Punctuality, reticence, public hygiene, independent thinking and exercise of judgment, and several other things I owe to my association with them."

His attitude is epitomized in words uttered shortly after the passing of the Independence Resolution:

> Whatever I do and whatever happens, my English friends will accept my word that, whilst I am impatient to break the British bondage, I am no enemy of Britain.

In spite of some unhappy bitterness and intolerance on both sides, there has been much friendliness between the English officials and the Satyagrahis, of which the following charming incident may be taken as a sample. After Mahadev Desai, Gandhi's devoted secretary and disciple, had been arrested, he was visited by Mirabhen (Miss Slade) and told her his story; which was related in *Young India* by Miss Slade.

> The trial was over (he said) and I was put into the prison van. On the back of the van was an English sergeant.

There was a huge crowd all round. Suddenly a stone was thrown from somewhere, and it hit the sergeant on the chin, giving him a nasty cut. "Ugh!" exclaimed the man, catching the stone as it fell from his face. "See what your wretched people do! If they stuck to non-violence we could have nothing to say. But look at this behaviour! People who can't be non-violent had better keep out of this movement or they will soon spoil it." I hastily expressed my sorrow (continued Mahadev) and told him that if he would stop the van, I would speak to the crowds and make them thoroughly ashamed of themselves. "No, I can't stop the van," said the sergeant, and again he began to complain of the affair. "But what can I do shut up in this van?" I said, "I can only assure you I am extremely pained at the incident, and I would gladly atone for it. Hit me with the stone—it will be good," I added. "No, no!" said the sergeant, beginning to melt. But after a little while he began again to get sore on the subject. . . .

Once more he looked at the stone that was in his hand and remarked, "I shall keep this as a memento." "No, please, don't do that," I said. "If you have any belief in the sincerity of my sorrow, you will throw it away." This suddenly touched his heart, and then and there he threw it from him!

We were now passing by the Ashram. "See, there's my house," I said, pointing it out to him. "That's nice," he replied, "I have never seen the Ashram. When you come out of prison I must come and visit you." "Yes, do," I said, "I should be delighted. And perhaps now you would give me your name, that I may keep it by me?" "Yes, certainly, but I've not got a pencil to write it down with," he remarked. "Here is my pen," I replied, handing it to him through the wire netting. He wrote down his name, and with the piece of paper was about to hand back the pen through the netting. "No, please keep the pen," I said, "it will be a nice memento, and how much better than the stone." He was deeply touched, and with overflowing appreciations put the little souvenir away in his pocket.

We parted the very best of friends, concluded Mahadev, his face beaming with delight.

It is important to remember these things. Englishmen should see in Mahatma Gandhi their truest friend. If he takes away their Empire, he will at least restore to them their soul. It may be that he will infect them with his own grandeur and generosity of outlook. Least of all should they be afraid of the Indian Movement. I have surely said enough to show that—in Gandhi's own words—

Indian Nationalism is not exclusive, nor aggressive, nor destructive. It is health-giving, religious, and therefore humanitarian.

XV

The Social Awakening

As Mahatma Gandhi and his band of pilgrims made their romantic and historic march through the villages of Gujerat towards the sea, he preached at every stopping-place certain urgent duties of the New India. One of these was the removal of untouchability and care for the poor; another was the abolition of the liquor traffic: a third was the promotion of Khadi, the most intimate symbol of the new spirit; and the fourth was the complete emancipation of women. Let us examine these four things in turn, for they will give us a vivid picture of the national awakening which Mahatma Gandhi has inspired.

XVI

The Poor

Perhaps the most attractive feature of the Nationalist Movement is the fact that it is so largely directed by love of the poor and aimed at relieving their distress. We have seen Gandhi's own love of poverty earlier in this chapter. He aims at inspiring this same love (and love of poverty always means love of the poor) in his followers.

"There is no worship purer or more pleasing to God than selfless service of the poor."

"God dwells among the poor as they cling to Him as their sole refuge and shelter. To serve the poor is therefore to serve Him."

Of the peasants of Champaran, Gandhi said that in meeting them he was face to face with God, Ahimsa, and Truth. But it is not only Gandhi in whom this love of the poor is active. It is alive, a constant flame, in the great heart of Sardar Vallabhbhai Patel. "If any one," he has said, "is fit to walk with his head erect on this earth, it is the peasant. He is the producer, the others are parasites." "Where is there another so honest as a peasant, so free from bad habits and vices, so guileless, so God-fearing, living in the sweat of his brow?"

"The future of India lies with the peasantry," says the socialist and republican Pandit Jawaharlal Nehru. We think of many others—some, like G. K. Devadhar and Professor Karve, not Congressmen (but devoted patriots all the same), who have given their lives to the care of the widows and to women's education. There are many like Amritlal V. Thakkar, the beloved "Bapa" (Father) of the Bhils, or Rajagopalacharya, a herald of the spinning-wheel in the South as a cure for India's poverty, or Rajendra Prasad, the noble guide of the peasants of Bihar. Some of the younger men are strong with the same ideal. V. A. Sundaram, taken before a magistrate in Madras in 1931, declared, "I have joined the movement simply because I love the poor. I worship them. They are the saviours of humanity. Let me feel blessed in their noble company. Let me live amongst them and share their joys and sorrows."

There need be no fear that the poor and the depressed classes will be exploited under a free India. Lord Lloyd has said that "Indian self-government must mean tyranny and chaos." "Every piece of moral reform in India, whether social, hygienic, educational, or administrative, would vanish in a night. They would let the jungle in again." That, as *The Church Times* rightly says, is nonsense.

Let us rather hear Gandhi's own forecast of the future: "The Swaraj of my—our—dream recognizes no race or religious distinctions. Nor is it to be the monopoly of the lettered persons nor yet of moneyed men. Swaraj is to be for all, including the former, but emphatically including the maimed, the blind, the starving toiling millions." "The Swaraj of my dream is the poor man's Swaraj."

In ten years Gandhi has done more for the peasants than the foreign Government has achieved in a century. He is still sending out missionaries on the hard crusade of village uplift. "I ask you," he said to his workers in Orissa, "to go to the villages and bury yourselves there, not as their masters or benefactors, but as their humble servants. Let them know what to do and how to change their modes of living from your daily conduct and way of living. . . . I ask you to go forth as messengers of God carrying balm for the wounded soul of India." In a recent address to the Labour Union of Ahmedabad, he said, "It is my fervent prayer to God that He may never separate me from you, and that I may lay down my life in the service of the poor."

Although the Declaration of Rights adopted by the National Congress at Karachi in March 1931 cannot be regarded as representing the considered mind of the Indian people, and although certain sections of it will no doubt prove impracticable in the working, it does indicate the deep concern of the Congress for the poor, and as a basis of a truly democratic state, should be received with joy and hope by every Christian. It runs as follows:

This Congress is of the opinion that to enable the masses to understand what the Swaraj as conceived by the Congress will mean to them, it is desirable to state the position of the Congress in a manner easily understood by them.

The Congress therefore declares that any constitution which may be agreed to on its behalf shall provide or enable the Swaraj Government to provide the following:

(1) The fundamental rights of the people, such as (A)

Freedom of association; (B) Freedom of speech and the press; (C) Freedom of conscience and the free profession and practice of religion subject to public order and morality; (D) Protection of the culture, language, and script of minorities; (E) Equal rights to the obligations of all citizens, without any bar on account of sex; (F) No disability to attach to any person by reason of religion, caste, or creed in regard to public employment, office of power or honour, and exercise of any trade or calling; (G) Equal rights of all citizens of access to and use of public roads, public wells, and all other places of public resort; (H) The right to keep and bear arms in accordance with the regulations and reservations made in that behalf; and (I) No person shall be deprived of his liberty, nor his dwelling or property be entered into, sequestered, or confiscated, save in accordance with the law.

(2) Religious neutrality on the part of the State.

(3) A living wage for industrial workers, limited hours of labour, healthy conditions of work, protection against the economic consequences of old age, sickness, and unemployment.

(4) Labour to be freed from serfdom or the conditions bordering on serfdom.

(5) Protection of women workers and specially adequate provision for leave during the maternity period.

(6) Prohibition against the employment of children of school-going age in factories.

(7) The right of labour to form Unions to protect their interests with suitable machinery for the settlement of disputes by arbitration.

(8) A substantial reduction of land revenues and agricultural rents paid by peasants in case of uneconomic holdings, exemption from rent for such period as may be necessary, relief being given to small Zamindars whenever necessary by reason of such reduction.

(9) The imposition of progressive income-tax on agricultural incomes above the fixed income.

(10) A graduated inheritance tax.

(11) Adult suffrage.

(12) Free primary education.

(13) Military expenditure to be reduced by at least one half of the present scale.

(14) Expenditures and salaries in the Civil Departments to be largely reduced.No servant of the State other than a specially employed expert and the like to be paid above a certain fixed figure which should not ordinarily exceed Rs. 500 per month.

(15) The protection of indigenous cloth by the exclusion of foreign cloth and foreign yarn from the country.

(16) Total prohibition of intoxicating drinks and drugs.

(17) No duty on salt.

(18) Control over Exchange and Currency policy so as to help Indian industries and bring relief to the masses.

(19) The control by the State of the key industries and mineral resources.

(20) The control of usury, direct or indirect.

Swaraj in fact is desired for the sake of the poor. "To the peasants," says Jawaharlal Nehru, "Swaraj is food and drink."

With this love of the poor there goes a natural desire to abolish untouchability. Most educated Indians share Gandhi's ideals in this respect, although it must be admitted that they are as yet far from being fulfilled in actual practice. Here are some of his many sayings on the subject:

Without the removal of the taint of untouchability, Swaraj is a meaningless term. Swaraj is as inconceivable without full reparation to the "depressed" classes as it is impossible without real Hindu-Moslem unity.

Untouchability is repugnant to reason and to the instinct of mercy, pity, and love.

No man can consider another man inferior to himself. He must consider every man as his blood-brother. It is the cardinal principle of every religion.

Gandhi is not content with mere sympathy, there must be action. He himself in the teeth of opposition took an "untouchable" family into his Ashram at Sabarmati. He always insists on the "untouchables" being given a good and equal place at his meetings. From his early days he has performed the "untouchable" duties of the sweeper. So once, when a municipality presented him with an address, which omitted any reference to his service of the "untouchables," he administered a stern rebuke, declaring that he himself was "a *bhangi*, a scavenger, a spinner, a weaver, and a labourer, and I want, if at all, to be honoured as such." Even loving service is not enough; we must identify ourselves with the "untouchables." It is not enough to open wells, temples, and schools to them. "You should love them even as yourselves so that the moment they see you they might feel that you are one of them." He has made the noble declaration, "I do not desire to be born again, but if I am really born again, I desire to be born amidst the untouchables, so as to share their difficulties and to work for their liberation."

Not only untouchability, but the breakdown of every form of rigid caste exclusiveness has been accelerated by the events of the last two years. Common suffering and a common ideal have brought all classes together. In the jails, members of all castes mixed freely and came to know and love one another. During the great Hijrat (Emigration) Movement in Gujerat, a wonderful spirit of friendliness was born of the universal suffering. In one village a Patidar (well-to-do farmer), a goldsmith, and a barber all took refuge in the house of a potter. I myself remember vividly being entertained to meals in a Hindu Temple. The party consisted of a Brahmin, a Patidar, a Bania (merchant), a Christian, and our Mohammedan motor-driver. "There was a time," says Jawaharlal Nehru, "when I used to call myself a Kashmiri Brahmin. I tried hard to forget it, and now I have almost forgotten it. I am only an Indian now."

XVII

The Abolition of the Liquor Traffic

All parties have combined to fight the drink traffic, which among the poor of India at least has a disastrous effect. The Congress has pledged itself to an advanced policy of Temperance Reform. Mahatma Gandhi has always believed in total abstinence, and recommends prohibition for India. And Dr. Ansari, the progressive Moslem leader, has said, "Forbidden by his religion to the Mussulman and held pernicious by the Hindu, the evil of drink would not have spread so rapidly and extensively, had the Government taken a sympathetic attitude towards those who were endeavouring to stop it."

All over the country, liquor shops have been vigorously picketed, and with great success. In some areas, the palms from which the toddy juice is taken, have been cut down. I saw something of this campaign in Ahmedabad at the end of 1930. Outside every shop there would be sitting two or three women, sometimes on chairs provided by the shopkeeper. Every one had a badge with a number and a book of printed forms. On these the names of all those who came to buy liquor were entered: the women tried to persuade them not to buy: and next day a letter, enclosing literature and some sort of "pledge" would be posted to them. Everything was carried on with the utmost possible courtesy and efficiency.

XVIII

The Khadi Movement

At least to Indian eyes, Khadi is one of the most significant signs of the awakening. As a remedy for the poverty of the peasants it is a symbol of the new love of the poor. The simple white dress, which is worn equally by all, is a token of the democratic spirit. Gandhi believes that there is no better means of discipline, of making the masses amenable to control, than the Gospel of Khadi. "The supreme value of Khadi," writes one of his followers, "lay in its capacity silently to induce this transformation of character, and that is why Khadi is so intimately related to Civil Disobedience."

Since Mahatma Gandhi's advocacy of the spinning-wheel has been a source of some bewilderment to his Western admirers, it may be well to set down here, in his own words, a few of the reasons for his enthusiasm.

1. Spinning helps to solve the problem of India's poverty.

"Hunger is the argument that is driving India to the

spinning-wheel. The call of the spinning-wheel is the noblest of all. Because it is the call of love. And love is Swaraj." "Without a cottage industry the Indian peasant is doomed. He cannot maintain himself from the produce of the land. He needs a supplementary industry. Spinning is the easiest, the cheapest and the best." "Hand-spinning does solve the problem of India's chronic poverty, and is an insurance against famine."

2. The spinning-wheel is a symbol of the unity of the rich and poor.

"I cannot conceive any higher way of worshipping God than by doing for the poor, in His name, the work they themselves do."

3. It is a symbol of all-India unity.

"For me the spinning-wheel and Khadi are the symbols of all-India unity; therefore I regard them as a national sacrament." "Hand-spinning means the greatest voluntary co-operation the world has ever seen. It means co-operation among millions of human beings scattered over a very wide area and working for their daily bread."

4. It is a symbol of love for the whole world.

"It is a symbol of love for mankind." "The Charkha is a symbol not of commercial war, but of commercial peace. It bears, not a message of ill will towards the nations of the earth but of good will and self-help. I may deserve the curses of posterity for many mistakes of omission and commission, but I am confident of its blessings for suggesting a revival of the Charkha. I stake my all on it. For every revolution of the wheel spins peace, good will, and love."

5. It is an ever-present spur to simplicity of life.

"There is one thing that may be truly said about the Khadi enterprise, in addition to its economic value—it brings us back to simplicity and self-reliance. 'If a man,' says the Chinese gardener-sage, 'has a machine-like heart in his breast, he has lost his grasp of pure unity, and becomes involved in complexity.'" "The spinning-wheel stands for a simple life and high thinking. It is a standing rebuke against the modern mad rush for adding material comfort upon comfort and making life so complicated as to make one doubly unfit for knowing oneself or one's God." . .

6. It is an invaluable discipline for the character.

"The Charkha is a symbol of simplicity, self-reliance, self-control." "It needs plodding. Ability to plod is Swaraj. It is Yoga. Nor need the reader be frightened of the monotony. Monotony is the law of nature. . . . The monotony of necessary occupations is exhilarating and life-giving. . . . And when India has monotonously worked away at turning out Swaraj, she will have produced a thing of beauty which will be a joy for ever. But it cannot be without the spinning-wheel. Therefore the best national education for India is undoubtedly an intelligent handling of the spinning-wheel."

7. It is a perfect cure for idleness.

"The central idea is not so much to carry on a commercial war against foreign countries as to utilize the idle hours of the nation, and thus by natural processes to help it to get rid of her growing pauperism." "Swaraj has no meaning for the millions if they do not know how to employ their enforced idleness."

8. It is very simple to learn.

"The beauty of spinning is that it is incredibly simple, easily learnt, and can be cheaply introduced."

9. Khadi has a high æsthetic value.

"To me Khadi is any day more artistic than the finest Dacca muslin, for its associations. Khadi supports to-day those who were starving. . . . Khadi, therefore, has a soul about it. It has an individuality about it." "The householder should train himself to see art and beauty in the spotlessly white Khadi and to appreciate its uneven softness."

10. Hand-spinning has a deep religious value.

"It will save our women from forced violation of their purity. It will, as it must, do away with begging as a means of livelihood. It will remove our enforced idleness. It will steady the mind. And I verily believe that when millions take to it as a sacrament, it will turn our faces Godward."

11. It is the secret of Swaraj.

"Swaraj is unattainable without the beautiful art of hand-spinning becoming universal in India." "If you want to feed the hungry, to clothe the naked, there is no other way out of the difficulty but spinning for the whole of India." "In hand-spinning is hidden the protection of women's virtue, the insurance against famine, and the cheapening of prices. In it is hidden the secret of Swaraj."

During 1930, according to the report of the All-India Spinners' Association, there was a remarkable progress in Khadi production, even though many of the leading workers in this field were put in jail. The total production increased by 68 per cent. over that of the previous year. Andhra, the Punjab, and Maharashtra more than doubled their output, and Delhi and Kashmir nearly doubled it. The United Provinces reached a figure three times that of the previous year. The Tamil Nad has always held the record for Khadi work and has maintained it. Bengal, having lost nearly all its chief workers to the jails, could not register any increase. The number of Khadi depots throughout India rose from 384 to 600. The production activities of the A.I.S.A. covered 6,494 villages, and found employment for 139,969 spinners, 11,426 weavers, and 1,006 carders. These figures are important as showing that Gandhi's emphasis on Khadi is not merely an idle dream, but is a practical and effective way of solving the problem of unemployment and starvation.

XIX

The Movement of the Women

The Women's Movement, which has been slowly progressing for fifty years, has received an enormous impetus in the last twelve months. "Mahatma Gandhi," says Mr. C. R. Reddy, "has produced an explosion of the pent-up woman power of India which is nothing short of a miracle." The women of India insisted on taking a full share in the Satyagraha struggle of 1930. Thousands of them went to jail. Many exposed themselves without flinching to the sticks and lathis of the police. Others toured the country on Khadi propaganda. Their chief work, however, was the picketing of liquor shops and foreign cloth centres. In Gandhi's view, indeed, women—because of their strong but gentle nature—are the natural disciples of Satyagraha. "If non-violence is the law of our being, the future is with woman." Sardar Vallabhbhai Patel also specially looked for support to the women of Gujerat, since they excelled men in simplicity, purity, and steadfastness of purpose, which are the weapons of non-violent warfare. His trust was more than justified on the day when a huge procession of 1,500 women walked quietly through the streets of Borsad to receive without fear or retaliation an assault of beating and abuse from the police. Their leader, covered with her blood-stained garments, walked bravely on, repeating the Holy Name of God, to receive still further blows.

Some remarkable instances may be cited of the effects of the Movement.

At Patna, in July last year, about twenty women, belonging to the chief families of the town, who were still in purdah, came forward for the picketing of foreign cloth shops. A great procession of women, young and old, of every caste, went through the city, many of them never having appeared in public in their lives. In Meerut, in order to walk in a procession as a protest against Gandhi's arrest, 5,000 women came out of purdah and never returned to it.

One day in Bombay a young Congress worker, Babu Ganu, was killed while offering Satyagraha by lying in front of a motor wagon full of foreign piece-goods, and by his death became a national hero. The effect was revolutionary. As the great procession that accompanied his body to the burning-place passed through the crowded streets of Bombay, people saw with astonishment that Hindu women (who never attend funerals) were carrying the bier along with the men. And although no Hindu woman may light the pyre even of her husband, father or brother, it was a Brahmin woman of a most exclusive family that set fire to the pyre of this Kamati boy.

At Munshiganj, the "untouchables" had been offering Satyagraha outside the Kali Temple for over nine months. At last some of them went on hunger-strike. In order to save their lives, two hundred high-caste women armed themselves with saws, axes, and hammers, stormed the Temple, broke down the barriers that protected it, and threw it open to their "untouchable" brothers.

"When the story of this Movement comes to be written," says Mahatma Gandhi, "the sacrifices made by the women of India will occupy the foremost place."

The future is indeed full of hope. Dr. Muthulakshmi Reddy, the first woman member of a Legislative Council (of which she was elected Deputy-President) in India, has pointed out that Indian women have had the generous support of Indian men in the reforms. "When India secures self-government," she says, "there is not the least doubt that Indian women will very soon get rid of all their disabilities, such as the customs of early marriage, purdah, unequal marriage laws, unjust inheritance laws, etc," which have persisted too long owing to the illiteracy of the masses (which under Swaraj will be remedied) and the neutrality of Government towards social evils.

XX

We can best conclude this chapter by quoting two recent estimates of Gandhi's influence. The first is from a somewhat critical account by Sir Francis Younghusband, in his *Dawn in India*.

"I believe that Gandhi has done India four great services. Firstly, he has instilled courage into India and made Indians feel their manhood. Secondly, he has aroused in them a sense of nationhood. Thirdly, he has stressed the importance of religion in the national life, denounced materialism, and emphasized the value of spiritual things. Lastly, he has brought to India the attention of the whole world, till every nation is now interested in what is going on in India."

The second is from the more enthusiastic pen of Dr. Will Durant. In his *Case for India*, he summarizes the "astonishing record of Gandhi's achievements" as follows:

"First, through leaping far ahead of the moral consciousness of mankind, which is yet tribal and national, he has helped the international organization of industries and States to prepare us for the larger morality, in which the code of conduct between gentlemen will be—because world order will necessitate it—applied to the conduct of nations. Second, he has given life and meaning to a Christianity which had become, among ourselves, mere poetry and pretence; he has lifted it to a plane where the most unscrupulous statesman must reckon with it as a great force; he has ennobled it beyond modern precedent by unconsciously attaching to its banner one-fifth of the human race. Third, he has for a generation kept a great revolutionary movement from all but sporadic violence.... He has approached one of the fundamental principles of statesmanship, to persuade radicals that change must be gradual in order to be permanent, and to persuade conservatives that change must be. Fourth, he has educated his people; he has aroused them, as no man before in their history, to the evils of untouchability, temple prostitution, child marriage, unmarriageable widows, and the traffic in opium. Fifth, and despite his partial defence of that caste system which perpetually divides and weakens India, he has, by the power of imagination and the word, given to India a psychological unity never possessed by it before, making all these races, languages, and creeds feel and think alike, as the prelude to united action. Sixth, he has given to his countrymen what they needed above everything else—pride. They are no longer hopeless or supine; they are prepared for danger and responsibility, and therefore for freedom."

CHAPTER III

THE MEANING OF SATYAGRAHA

"He who chooses to avenge wrong with hatred is assuredly wretched. But he who strives to conquer hatred with love fights his battle in joy and confidence; he withstands many as easily as one, and has very little need of fortune's aid. Those whom he vanquishes yield joyfully, not through failure, but through increase in their power."—SPINOZA

I

Probably the most original and significant of all Mahatma Gandhi's contributions to the thought of the world will be found in his idea of Satyagraha,[1] or non-violent resistance, as a weapon to be used not only by individuals, but also to settle international disputes. He does not, indeed, claim to have originated the idea, or to have any patent for its use; he compares himself rather to the "keeper of the lighthouse called Satyagraha" in the otherwise chartless sea of Indian politics. He is simply the humble, but devoted, servant of the great principle, "for which I live, for which I desire to live, for which I believe I am equally prepared to die."

In this chapter we will attempt to describe the

[1] *Satyagraha* is the principle which means "soul-force," or "truth-force." *Satyagraha* presupposes the living presence and guidance of God. The leader depends not on his own strength but on that of God. He acts as the voice within guides him. Very often, therefore, what are practical politics so-called are unrealities to him, though in the end his prove to be the most practical politics. A *Satyagrahi* is a person who believes in this principle and puts it into practice.

ideal and method of Satyagraha, and we will give some historical examples of its use. At the end we will consider whether it may not prove to be that moral substitute for war for which William James and others have pleaded. Some account of Satyagraha is of real importance in a book of this kind. There is no stronger argument for India's freedom than the method by which she has striven to attain it. All the qualities which fit a nation for self-government have been displayed in the Satyagraha campaigns. There is no Hindu-Moslem problem among the disciples of Satyagraha; the minorities have no fear that their just claims will be ignored; in the possession of this all-powerful weapon of defence, India can regard the reduction of the army estimates with equanimity. No Empire has any right to keep in bondage a nation which is able to produce so convincing an evidence of a lofty and spiritual civilization. Satyagraha may yet prove to be the most perfect flower of the ancient culture of India, and her finest gift to the life and thought of the world.

There are two ways of carrying on a struggle, says Mr. C. R. Reddy, late Vice-Chancellor of the Andrha University, by the destruction of the opponent or by his conversion. "The method inaugurated by Jesus Christ is conversion by self-suffering." Mahatma Gandhi has claimed Jesus Christ as the prince of Satyagrahis, a title which he has also given to "the thousands of devout Christians in the early days of Christianity" for their "patient suffering of oppression."

The original source of the idea of Satyagraha came first from a beautiful Gujerati poem:

> If a man gives you a drink of water and you give him a drink in return, that is nothing. Real beauty consists in doing good against evil,

and then from the Sermon on the Mount. "It was the New Testament," says Gandhi, "which really awakened me to the rightness and value of Passive Resistance. When I read in the Sermon on the Mount such passages as 'Resist not him that is evil; but whosoever smiteth thee on thy right cheek, turn to him the other also,' and 'Love your enemies; pray for them that persecute you, that ye may be the sons of your Father which is in heaven,' I was simply overjoyed, and found my opinion confirmed where I least expected it. The *Bhagavadgita* deepened the impression, and Tolstoy's *The Kingdom of God is within You* gave it a permanent form."

Satyagraha is therefore the transformation of war by the spirit of Jesus. It is the specifically religious method of settling disputes or righting wrongs. The idea is very simple. Whereas in ordinary conflict we try to get our own way by attacking our opponents, in Satyagraha we try to get the way of Truth by attacking ourselves. "In Satyagraha," says Gandhi, "we expect to win over our opponents by self-suffering, that is, by love." This is not a mere passive acceptance of suffering; it is a positive adventure of love which seeks, not to destroy the opponent, but to effect in him a change of heart, thus leaving him stronger and better than he was. It is "a most powerful expression of soul-anguish, and an eloquent protest against the continuance of an evil state." It is indeed a protest, but it is a protest which employs no violence in thought, word, or deed. Richard Gregg, in his remarkable *Psychology and Strategy of Gandhi's Non-Violent Resistance* has called Satyagraha "a sort of moral ju-jitsu." In ju-jitsu a very common method of throwing an opponent is suddenly to abandon all resistance and to pull him over towards you. In the same way, "the non-violence and good will of the victim act like the lack of physical opposition by the user of physical ju-jitsu, to cause the attacker to lose his moral balance. He suddenly and unexpectedly loses the moral support which the usual violent resistance of most victims would render him. He plunges forward, as it were, into a new world of values. He feels helpless and insecure because of the novelty of the situation and his ignorance as to how to handle it. The principle of surprise, so potent in warfare, has made him lose his poise and self-confidence. The victim not only lets the attacker come, but, as it were, jerks him forward by kindness, generosity, and good will, so that the attacker quite loses his moral balance. The user of non-violent resistance, knowing what he is doing and having a more creative purpose and perhaps a clearer sense of ultimate values than the other, retains his moral balance. He uses the leverage of a superior wisdom to subdue the rough direct force or physical strength of his opponent."

At the beginning of the Movement in South

Africa, Mahatma Gandhi used to call his great ideal by the name "passive resistance." But this carried with it implications alien to his mind, nor was it satisfactory to have only an English expression that could not pass as current coin in the Indian community. A small prize was announced in *Indian Opinion* for the best suggestion of an alternative word. Maganlal Gandhi suggested "Sadagaha," meaning "firmness in a good cause." The Mahatma liked the word, but thought it was not wide enough, and corrected it to "Satyagraha." *Satya* (Truth) implies love, and *Agraha* (Firmness) engenders and therefore serves as a synonym for force. Satyagraha represents therefore the Force which is born of Truth and Love or non-violence.

II

Satyagraha can take many different forms, provided always that the cause is just, the inspiration Truth, and the method perfect non-violence and love. Mahatma Gandhi was once asked to define the meaning of Satyagraha and its various branches, and he did so at length in *Young India* of March 21, 1921. We shall give the passage in full, as it will make clear much of what is to follow.

Satyagraha is literally holding on to Truth, and it means, therefore, Truth-force. Truth is soul or spirit. It is, therefore, known as soul-force. It excludes the use of violence because man is not capable of knowing the absolute truth and, therefore, not competent to punish. The word was coined in South Africa to distinguish the non-violent resistance of the Indians of South Africa from the contemporary "passive resistance" of the suffragettes and others. It is not conceived as a weapon of the weak.

Passive resistance is used in the orthodox English sense and covers the suffragette movement as well as the resistance of the Nonconformists. Passive resistance has been conceived and is regarded as a weapon of the weak. Whilst it avoids violence, being not open to the weak, it does not exclude its use if, in the opinion of the passive resister, the occasion demands it. However, it has always been distinguished from armed resistance, and its application was at one time confined to the Christian martyrs.

Civil Disobedience is civil breach of unmoral statutory enactments. The expression was, so far as I am aware, coined by Thoreau to signify his own resistance to the laws of a slave state. He has left a masterly treatise on the duty of Civil Disobedience. But Thoreau was not perhaps an out-and-out champion of non-violence. Probably, also, Thoreau limited his breach of statutory laws to the Revenue Law, i.e. payment of taxes, whereas the term Civil Disobedience, as practised in 1919, covered a breach of any statutory and unmoral law. It signified the resister's outlawry in a civil, i.e. non-violent, manner. He invoked the sanctions of the law and cheerfully suffered imprisonment. It is a branch of Satyagraha.

Non-Co-operation predominantly implies withdrawing of co-operation from the State that in the Non-Co-operator's view has become corrupt and excludes Civil Disobedience of the fierce type described above. By its very nature, Non-Co-operation is even open to children of understanding, and can be safely practised by the masses. Civil Disobedience presupposes the habit of willing obedience to laws without fear of their sanctions. It can therefore be practised only as a last resort and by a select few in the first instance, at any rate. Non-Co-operation, too, like Civil Disobedience, is a branch of Satyagraha, which includes all non-violent resistance for the vindication of Truth."

III

The particular form in which Satyagraha may be expressed is not, however, of great importance. The essential thing is the spiritual principle which underlies it. That principle is that Truth should be its foundation and Love its methods. Satyagraha can thus only be offered in a righteous cause, and will succeed only in so far as its votaries observe righteousness and truth.

"Satyagrahis may rest assured, that even if there is only one among them who is pure as crystal, his sacrifice suffices to achieve the end in view. The world rests upon the bedrock of *Satya* or truth. *Asatya* meaning untruth also means non-existent, and *Satya* or truth also means that which *is*. If untruth does not so much as exist, its victory is out of the question. And truth being that which *is* can never be destroyed. This is the doctrine of Satyagraha in a nutshell."

In other words, we live in a moral universe, and if we base our cause on morality, that is, in disciplined love and perfect truth, it is bound to triumph. For love and truth are alike invincible.

"Satyagraha is love. The law of love—call it attraction, affinity, cohesion, if you like—governs the world. Life persists in face of death. The universe continues in spite of destruction continually going on. Truth triumphs over untruth. Love conquers hate. God eternally triumphs over Satan."

"In true Satyagraha there is neither disappointment nor defeat. As truth is all-powerful, Satyagraha can never be defeated." Thus the injunction "Love your enemies" is not only the noblest idealism; it is also the most practical politics. "The one permissible way of convincing our enemy is by friendliness and kindness." India must conquer her "so-called conquerors by love." "My Non-Co-operation has its root not in hatred but in love." At the beginning of the 1930 struggle, Gandhi reiterated his simple creed of love. "I embark upon the campaign," he declared, "as much out of my love for the Englishman as for the Indian. By self-suffering I seek to convert him, never to destroy him." In the first letter to the Viceroy in 1930, Gandhi clearly stated the aim of Satyagraha. "My ambition is no less than to convert the British people through non-violence, and thus make them see the wrong they have done to India." "I do not seek," he continued, "to harm your people. I want to serve my own. . . . If I have equal love for your people with mine it will not long remain hidden. . . . If the people join me, as I expect they will, the sufferings they will undergo, unless the British nation sooner retraces its steps, will be enough to melt the stoniest hearts."

"A Satyagrahi," he says again, "never desires to reach the goal by harbouring or increasing ill will or hatred against his opponent." Satyagraha is the law of love and hence the law of life itself. "Love does not burn others, it burns itself. Therefore a Satyagrahi will joyfully suffer even unto death." It follows therefore that a Satyagrahi, "whilst he will strain every nerve to compass the end of the existing rule, will do no intentional injury in thought, word, or deed to the person of a single Englishman." There is no room for hatred in Satyagraha. It has not yet achieved its crowning victories, because men have not yet shed hatred. Satyagraha does not, however, imply a sentimental ignoring of vital wrongs. It does not cry Peace, Peace, where there is no peace. It must fearlessly face hatred and wrong, and make known the evils which it would destroy. It is an active force; but its force is the force of love.

IV

Since love is the inspiration of Satyagraha, it follows that it is an essentially active and positive weapon, to be used not as the last despairing expedient of the weak, but as the expression of the restrained energy of the strong. As we have seen, it is not the same as passive resistance.

At a meeting in Germiston, one of the magnates of Johannesburg delivered a speech in support of Gandhi, but described the Transvaal Indians as having "taken to passive resistance which is a weapon of the weak." This was felt by Gandhi to be a misrepresentation of his position. He is anxious to stress the distinction between passive resistance and Satyagraha. There is no room for love in passive resistance, but it is the ruling principle of Satyagraha. There is, in passive resistance, always a possible resort to arms; "Satyagraha and brute force, being each a negation of the other, can never go together."

"In passive resistance there is always present an idea of harassing the other party and there is a simultaneous readiness to undergo any hardship entailed upon us by such activity; while in Satyagraha there is not the remotest idea of injuring the opponent. Satyagraha postulates the conquest of the adversary by suffering in one's own person."

Richard Gregg has emphasized this point. The conduct of the Satyagrahi, he says, "is not one of mere passive waiting or endurance. Toward his opponent he is not aggressive physically, but his mind and emotions are exceedingly active, wrestling constantly with the problem of persuading the latter that he is mistaken, seeking proposals as to a better way out, examining his own cause and organization to see what mistakes or short-sightedness there may be in them, thinking constantly of all the possible ways of winning the truth for both sides."

The words "passive" or "resistance" are indeed largely misleading in reference to Satyagraha. Satyagraha is essentially an active *force*. though it is force of an altogether new and spiritual quality. "Satyagraha is soul-force, pure and simple." It is love-force, the force that has no taint of violence. Non-violence in the form of love is the most active force in the world.

V

It is obviously no easy matter to practise Satyagraha. A high standard of ideal and conduct is demanded of its followers. In the first place, the

Satyagrahi must have a deep respect for law as such. "Before one can be fit for the practice of civil disobedience one must have rendered a willing and respectful obedience to the State laws." Very few men do this, specially in respect of those laws which do not involve any moral principle. An honest citizen who would not dream of committing theft will have no scruple about riding a bicycle in the dark without a lamp, if he can do so without incurring prosecution. But this is not the Satyagrahi's attitude to law. "A Satyagrahi obeys the laws of society intelligently and of his own free will, because he considers it his sacred duty to do so. It is only when a person has thus obeyed the laws of society scrupulously that he is in a position to judge as to which particular rules are good and just, and which unjust and iniquitous. Only then does the right accrue to him of the civil disobedience of certain laws in well-defined circumstances."

Then, since mass Satyagraha is national self-purification, every Satyagrahi "has to observe perfect chastity, adopt poverty, follow truth, and cultivate fearlessness." Those alone can follow this path "who are free from fear whether as to their possessions, false honour, their relatives, the Government, bodily injuries, death.

The Satyagrahi must be courteous, sympathetic, ever ready to believe the best. Shortly after the Truce of 1931, Mahatma Gandhi said to those of his followers who were disappointed at its terms:

"The Satyagrahi, whilst he is ever ready for war, must be equally eager for peace. He must welcome any honourable opportunity for peace. . . . Whilst a Satyagrahi never yields to panic or hesitancy, neither does he think of humiliating the other party, of reducing it to an abject surrender. He may not swerve from the path of justice and may not dictate impossible terms. He may not pitch his demands too high, neither may he pitch them too low. . . . A Satyagrahi has infinite patience, abundant faith in others, and ample hope."

Since Satyagraha is the way of Truth, "a Satyagrahi has no secrets to keep from his opponent or so-called enemy." "Satyagraha abhors secrecy. It is the openest form of warfare I have known. Similarly Satyagraha abhors cowardice, and he who preaches it with any selfishness about him damns himself." "A Satyagrahi may not resort to surreptitious practices. All that the Satyagrahis do can and must only be done openly."

Gregg has described the character of the Satyagrahi as follows: "He must have primarily that disposition best known as love—an interest in people so deep, and determined, and lasting as to be creative; a profound knowledge of or faith in the ultimate possibilities of human nature; a courage based probably upon a conscious or subconscious realization of the underlying unity of all life and eternal values or eternal life of the human spirit; a strong and deep desire for and love of truth; and a humility which is not cringing or self-deprecatory or timid, but rather a true sense of proportion in regard to people, things, qualities and ultimate values."

VI

Satyagraha is, in fact, essentially a spiritual weapon. Satyagraha, says Gandhi, "is a purely religious instrument, and its use therefore is possible only in men religiously inclined." His ideal indeed represents "an attempt to revolutionize the political outlook, it is an attempt to spiritualize our politics." In his deeply interesting and significant book, *Satyagraha in South Africa*, he has given the name of *dharmayuddha* (righteous war) to his campaign. This is not the same as the Holy War of the past, in which countless souls were massacred in the name of a particular religion. It is rather a war fought according to the universal principles of all religions; it is not so much a Holy War as a war for holiness. It is above all a struggle in the spiritual realm.

"In a righteous struggle God Himself plans campaigns and conducts battles. A *dharmayuddha*, in which there are no secrets to be guarded, no scope for cunning, and no place for untruth, comes unsought, and a man of religion is ever ready for it. A *dharmayuddha* can only be waged in the name of God, and it is only when the Satyagrahi feels quite helpless, is apparently on his last legs and finds utter darkness all around him, that God comes to the rescue. God helps when one feels oneself humbler than the very dust under one's feet. Only to the weak and helpless is divine succour vouchsafed."

Later, at the height of the Bardoli Satyagraha of 1928, Mahatma Gandhi wrote: "The fact is that Satyagraha presupposes the living presence and guidance of God. The leader depends not on his own strength, but on that of God. He acts as the voice within guides him. Very often, therefore, what are practical politics so-called are unrealities to him, though in the end his prove to be the most practical politics." A Satyagrahi is to remember that since he is fighting a battle for Truth, it is to the ultimate Truth, that is, to God, that he must look for strength.

"A Satyagrahi has no power he can call his own. All the power he may seem to possess is from and of God. . . . Without the help of God he is lame, blind, groping!"

When he was anticipating his arrest in 1930, Gandhi told his followers not to be disturbed if he was taken away, for, he said, "It is not I, but God who is guiding this Movement. He ever dwells in the hearts of all and He will vouchsafe to us the right guidance if only we have faith in Him."

To Gandhi, and to many of his followers, it is the spiritual triumph that is far more important than material success. At the end of the Bardoli Satyagraha, Gandhi wrote of Sardar Vallabhbhai Patel, who led the peasants to victory: "We have rightly honoured Vallabhbhai over the Bardoli victory. But you may not know his greater victory. Vallabhbhai realized Vallabha (God) in Bardoli. He saw that nothing but faith in God could keep together the thousands of men and women bound to their pledge. It is through religion that he found his approach to the hearts of those simple illiterate men and women."

There were some beautiful examples of this pure

and lofty religious spirit in the 1930 campaign. I would first quote the prayer used by the veteran Moslem leader, Mr. Abbas Tyabji, at the prayers preceding the raid on Government salt-works which led to his arrest:

> In Thy name, O God, we launch forth to-day. Give us strength to go on, to endure all sufferings with a smiling countenance and a heart singing forth Thy praise. Illumine us with Thy wisdom, and purge our heart of all ill will and hatred. Let not a single unworthy act stain our record. Guide our opponents also into the right path and bless them. Bless also our undertaking, for it is Thy promise that the cause of righteousness and truth always triumphs.

One of the women volunteers of Gujerat was beaten and insulted by the police. But all she could say was, "For a while I was even angry a little at the Sub-Inspector, but a little later I realized my mistake, as he was after all a brother to me."

It was my privilege to see something of the peasant farmers of Gujerat who left their homes and all their property and migrated to little huts in Baroda territory. I can testify to the beautiful spirit that dwelt among them. In one of the emigration camps, I listened to a moving address on Love by an ex-Deputy Collector who, after twenty-six years of loyal service, had resigned his post as a protest against the police atrocities, thereby forfeiting his pension. In another of the camps I heard an old man declare, "In ancient days, our Bhaktas had faith in God and saw Him face to face. We must have a faith like theirs. For everything depends on God."

Perhaps Mahatma Gandhi strikes the deepest note of all when he insists that *Swaraj* can only come through self-purification. "None can officiate at the altar of Swaraj who do not approach it with a pure hand and a pure heart."

The words "Self-purification" and "Self-sacrifice" run as an unfailing under-rhythm to all Gandhi's teaching. "God insists on the purity of the cause and an adequate sacrifice therefore." *The Church Times* in a striking article on "The Significance of Gandhi," says: "In Russia a new society is being evolved with persecution, killing, and the preaching of hatred. In Italy, a new society is developing under the protection of distinctly coercive measures. In India, men and women are being taught that if they would be free, they must first be good."

As we said at the beginning of this chapter, the Satyagraha Movement represents the application of the teaching and spirit of Jesus to the spheres of politics and international relations. The teaching of Satyagraha which we have just outlined might well come from some Fifth Gospel, in which the social and political life of the Kingdom of God had been described. During the last year, these principles have been put to a supreme test, and it is to the highest interest of Christians everywhere (provided that they are convinced of the justice of the cause) to help by prayer and by active propaganda and support to see that they advance to a successful conclusion. The Indian situation, says Dr. Will Durant in his *Case for India*, "represents the most extensive effort ever made to test the practicability of Christianity. If India should succeed, the stock of Christianity (by which we mean here the ethical ideals of Christ) would rise throughout the world; courtesy and peace would be in good repute unparalleled. Every moral ideal would be reinvigorated and perhaps the age of cynicism and despondency in which we live would come to an end. As Gandhi himself has said: 'If the Indian movement is carried to success on a non-violent basis, it will give a new meaning to patriotism, and, if I may say so in all humility, to life itself.' Yes, life would be dearer to us, it would again have significance beyond ourselves, if India should win."

VII

We should notice one final point. Since Satyagraha means national purification, it is normally accompanied by social reform and social service. In South Africa, Gandhi founded the Phœnix Ashram and the Tolstoy farm to be training-centres of Satyagraha and service. In Champaran, Gandhi's offering of Civil Disobedience was followed by an intensive campaign of village education. After the Bardoli Satyagraha, Gandhi told his followers at Surat, "Satyagraha includes civil disobedience, civil resistance to the tyranny of blind authority, but the capacity of resistance presupposes self-purification and constructive work." The tremendous stores of energy and enthusiasm created by the campaign had to be used in the purification of the whole district. "True Satyagraha is impossible without self-purification." In Bardoli itself he reminded the peasants that Swaraj could not be attained only by fighting. He quoted Garibaldi, who "drove the plough and tilled the soil just like an ordinary peasant whenever he could get respite from fighting." And General Botha was "a farmer among farmers like any in Bardoli." General Smuts was famous for his fruit orchard. "Driving out the English will not by itself establish Swaraj in India." That will only come with the solution of all internal problems. He urged the peasants to press forward with constructive work, to rid themselves of social abuses, to take up spinning, remove drink, attend to village sanitation, to have a properly managed school in every village, and to befriend the depressed classes.

VIII

Such are the main principles of Satyagraha. Are they really capable of a world-wide application? Are there no dangers in a weapon so accessible and so easy to use? Mr. Jamshed Mehta, the Lord Mayor of Karachi, a follower of Mahatma Gandhi, has recently drawn attention to certain of these dangers.

"The taste of the blood—breaking laws—has been so attractive that one finds to-day this blessed Satyagraha on the lips of everyone. As soon as you differ anywhere, be it in a school, in a house, in a group, in a circle of friends, in business, in an office, you find immediately threat of Satyagraha pointed at you. Between employer and employee, landlord and tenant, parents and children, teachers and pupils, brothers and friends, everywhere this pointed bayonet of Satyagraha seems to be ready for use. To break laws and rules of society or of the State seems to be so easy and handy. If a college professor suggests discipline, if a municipal officer recommends an extra tax, if children are requested not to make a noise, if hawkers are told to remove obstructions on roads, if changes or transfers are being arranged, if anything is done which does not suit anybody else, there is this dagger of Satyagraha pointed at you. Discrimination where to use and how to use seems to have been entirely lost in the whole nation, and this is a danger signal for any nation or country. It is exactly like an aeroplane, which is being used generally to fly from one country to another speedily, and is also used for throwing bombs. It is exactly like matches, which give light, and are also used for burning a house. One can clearly see this danger signal in the Satyagraha weapon also. Satyagraha can be used to advantage, but it can also be misused to entire destruction. I feel that unless those who proclaim Satyagraha as the best weapon to the wide world feel their responsibility in this matter, they will soon find the tables turned not only against themselves but on the whole country. If I can humbly suggest, I feel that some of the rigidly trained leaders, free from hatred, should now do nothing else but pass some years of their lives in each province and in each city and village to make people understand what real Satyagraha or true non-violence means, how it can be brought into operation, and when it ought to be brought into operation. I would humbly suggest a regular school of non-violence in every province, where high-minded souls who thoroughly understand this subject scientifically and religiously ought to be teachers to the students of politics, who in return should be kept as all-time workers to go round the country to give this message and teach what it is in reality. This can be the only safeguard for saving the country in my opinion."

This suggestion of Satyagraha-education is of vital importance. Mahatma Gandhi had himself urged it years before in South Africa. "Satyagraha is the noblest and best education. . . . It should be an essential of real education that a child should learn that in the struggle of life it can easily conquer hate by love, untruth by truth, violence by self-suffering." Satyagraha should hold as prominent a place in the education of every Indian child as the teaching of militarism used to be given in the Public Schools of England during the Great War. It should be included in every curriculum as a compulsory subject. Only thus can the dangers pointed out by Mr. Jamshed Mehta be avoided. But I believe that they can thus be avoided and that a nation which is adequately educated in Satyagraha will have no rivals; it will be the strongest and noblest nation upon earth.

IX

South Africa

Without attempting to write a history of Satyagraha, let us look back and see how far its principles have been practicable in the movements of the last quarter of a century.

Mahatma Gandhi practised Satyagraha in South Africa for no less than eight years. It was there that the idea came to birth, that it found its proper name, and was first tested. We do not propose to describe here the story of the long-drawn battle for the elementary human rights of Indians in South Africa, for it is familiar to every student of Indian affairs. Suffice it to say that the struggle was marked by the same zeal for self-purification, the same love of the poor, the same devotion to truth and non-violence that was later to be illustrated on so large a scale in India itself. Gandhi initiated the movement when in 1906 he took an oath not to submit to the Draft Asiatic Law Amendment Ordinance, which struck at the very existence of the Indians in South Africa. Later, he led the agitation against the £3 tax, against the decision of the Supreme Court dishonouring Indian marriages, against the law prohibiting Indians to enter the Transvaal. He roused to action the free and indentured workers throughout Natal, organized the Indian women into a non-violent army, and led the huge march of workers into the Transvaal and thence to prison. This agitation awoke the greatest interest in India, which culminated in the famous speech of Lord Hardinge in which he demanded a Commission of Inquiry. At last the "Indians' Relief Bill" was passed which abolished some of the worst of the conditions which were then existing. If to-day the horizon is again clouded, it is because—as Gandhi says—the spirit of Satyagraha is no longer universally active among the Indians of South Africa.

The South African movement illustrates very clearly some of the major principles of Satyagraha. It was conceived as a sacrifice. When the women volunteers entered Natal without permits and were finally arrested at Newcastle, suffering even—in the case of Valliamma—to the death in jail, Gandhi wrote, "It was an absolutely pure sacrifice that was offered by these sisters, who were innocent of legal technicalities. . . . But they knew that a mortal blow was being aimed at the Indians' honour, and their going to jail was a cry of agony and prayer offered from the bottom of their heart, was in fact the purest of all sacrifices. Such heart prayer is always acceptable to God."

The South African Satyagraha was marked by a number of acts of quixotic chivalry which made a deep impression on the opponents of the Indian claims. For example, when the Indian labourers on the north coast went on strike, the planters at Mount Edgecombe would have suffered heavy losses if the sugar-cane that had been cut had not been brought to the mills and crushed. So twelve hundred Indians returned to the mills simply to finish this piece of work and then went back to the strike. On another occasion, when the Indian employees of the Durban Municipality struck work, those who were engaged in the sanitary services of the borough or as attendants on the patients in the hospitals were sent back to their duties so that there might be no outbreak of disease in the city and the sick might have all the aid necessary. "In every step that he takes," says Gandhi, "the Satyagrahi is bound to consider the position of his adversary."

But the most notable example of this chivalry which did a good deal to enhance the prestige of the Indians and to prepare a suitable atmosphere for a settlement was the occasion when there was a great strike of the European employees of the Union railways which was embarrassing the Government, and it was suggested that this was the strategic moment for the striking of a decisive blow. But Gandhi declared that to take advantage of the Government in this way would be contrary to the spirit of Satyagraha, and that if they did undertake any march or strike it would be at some other time when the railway trouble had ended. This chivalrous decision was widely appreciated. One of the secretaries of General Smuts jocularly said to Gandhi: "I do not like your people, and do not care to assist them at all. But what am I to do? You help us in our days of need. How can we lay hands upon you? I often wish you took to violence like the English strikers, and then we would know at once how to dispose of you. But you will not injure even the enemy. You desire victory by self-suffering alone and never transgress your self-imposed limits of courtesy and chivalry. And that is what reduces us to sheer helplessness." There could not be a better illustration of the psychological effect of Satyagraha upon an opponent.

Gandhi has also described the effect of the March to the Transvaal on the minds of General Smuts and his followers. "Our firmness was very distressing to General Smuts, coupled as it was with peacefulness, and he even said as much. How long can you harass a peaceful man? How can you kill the voluntarily dead? There is no zest in killing one who welcomes death and therefore soldiers are keen upon seizing the enemy alive. If the mouse did not flee before the cat, the cat would be driven to seek another prey. If all lambs voluntarily lay with the lion, the lion would be compelled to give up feasting upon lambs. Great hunters would give up lion hunting if the lion took to non-resistance, Our victory was implicit in our combination of the two qualities of non-violence and determination."

Looking back over the whole struggle, Mahatma Gandhi recorded some of his impressions as follows:

It is impossible for those who consider themselves to be weak to apply this force. Only those who realize that there is something in man which is superior to the brute nature in him and that the latter always yields to it, can effectively be Satyagrahis. This force is to violence, and therefore to all tyranny, all injustice, what light is to darkness. In politics its use is based upon the immutable maxim that government of the people is possible only so long as they consent either consciously or unconsciously to be governed. We did not want to be governed by the Asiatic Act of 1907 of the Transvaal, and it had to go before this mighty force. Two courses were opened to us—to use violence when we were called upon to submit to the Act, or to suffer the penalties prescribed under the Act, and thus to draw out and exhibit the force of the soul within us for a period long enough to appeal to the sympathetic chord in the governors or law-makers. We have taken long to achieve what we set about striving for. That was because our

Satyagraha was not of the most complete type. All Satyagrahis do not understand the full value of the force nor have we men who always from conviction refrain from violence. The use of this force requires the adoption of poverty, in the sense that we must be indifferent whether we have the wherewithal to feed or clothe ourselves. During the past struggle all passive resisters were not prepared to go to that length. Some again were only passive resisters so-called. They came without any conviction, often with mixed motives, less often with impure motives. Some even, while engaged in the struggle, would have resorted to violence except for most vigilant supervision. Thus it was that the struggle became prolonged; for the exercise of the purest Soul-Force in its perfect form brings about instantaneous relief. For this, prolonged training of the individual soul is an absolute necessity, so that a perfect passive resister has to be almost, if not entirely, a perfect man.

We cannot all suddenly become such men, but the greater the spirit of Satyagraha in us, the better men will we become. Its use, therefore, is I think indisputable, and it is a force which, if it became universal, would revolutionize social ideas and do away with despotisms and the ever-growing militarism under which the nations of the West are groaning and are being almost crushed to death.

X

Champaran

The movement for the relief of the tenants of the indigo-planters in Champaran is one of the earliest and purest examples of Satyagraha in India. Champaran, the ancient domain of King Janaka, was the centre of the indigo plantations managed by foreign traders who subjected the peasants to great injustice and indignity. There is no room here to describe all their wrongs, the majority of which were admitted by a subsequent Government inquiry; but the most notorious of them was the *tinkathia* system by which the peasant was legally obliged to plant three out of every twenty parts of his land with indigo for his landlord. By 1917, the wrongs of Champaran had become widely known and Mahatma Gandhi went to investigate them. The conduct of his inquiry provides a vivid object-lesson in the methods of Satyagraha. On arrival, Gandhi at once visited the authorities and told them what he was going to do. The Secretary of the Planters' Association and the Commissioner of the Division, however, both received him unsympathetically. He was then served with a notice to leave Champaran. The Mahatma refused to do so until his inquiry was finished, and he was thereupon summoned for trial. "That day," he has recalled, "was an unforgettable event in my life and a red-letter day for the peasants and for me." It was India's first object-lesson in Civil Disobedience. Gandhi's statement before the magistrate may be quoted as showing the reasons for his action and the ideals which inspired it. "I have entered the country," he said, "with motives of rendering humanitarian and national service. . . . I have no other motive and cannot believe that my coming can in any way disturb public peace and cause loss of life. . . . The administration, however, have thought differently. . . . As a law-abiding citizen my first instinct would be, as it was, to obey the order served upon me. But I could not do so without doing violence to my sense of duty to those for whom I came. . . . Amidst this conflict of duty I could only throw the responsibility of removing me from them on the administration. . . . It is my firm belief that in the complex constitution under which we are living the only safe and honourable course for a self-respecting man is, in the circumstances such as face me to-day, to do what I have decided to do, that is, to submit without protest to the penalty of disobedience. . . . I have disregarded the order served upon me not for want of respect for lawful authority, but in obedience to the higher law of our being, the voice of conscience."

Before sentence was given Government had ordered the case to be withdrawn, and the Collector wrote to the Mahatma saying that he was at liberty to conduct the proposed inquiry, and that he might count on whatever help he needed from the officials. The result may be briefly stated. The facts collected by Gandhi roused Government to action. A Committee was appointed of which he was a member, and this found in favour of the peasants, recommending that the planters should refund a portion of their exactions which the Committee had found to be unlawful. The *tinkathia* system, after a century's use, was abolished. To-day, writes that devoted and noble worker Rajendra Prasad, "the peasant of Champaran is as free as any other man in India can be in the present conditions to develop and improve himself and his surroundings." He has gained boldness, strength, and self-respect.

Let us remark the following things in reference to

this campaign. First, that Gandhi's trust in the righteousness of his cause was abundantly justified. Had he tamely submitted to the Magistrate's order and left Champaran, the peasants would never have had justice. Secondly, let us note the high level of openness and courtesy with which the campaign was conducted. The Mahatma informed the police of all his movements: he allowed C.I.D. officials to be present at his inquiry. He behaved with the utmost courtesy to the Commissioner, the Magistrate, and the planters, especially trying to make friends with those who maligned him. "I did not want to irritate the planters," he said, "but to win them over with gentleness." He wrote to the District Magistrate, "I am most anxious to continue and to increase the friendly spirit. I am straining every nerve so far as in me lies to so conduct my mission that nothing but good will should be left behind, when its labours are finished. . . . The mission is totally of peace. I cannot too often give the assurance that I bear no ill will against the planters."

Finally we may note that the Satyagraha as always was accompanied by a campaign of social service. It was not enough to free the peasants from the domination of the planters. "I became convinced that work of a permanent nature was impossible without proper village education." So primary schools were opened in six villages, sanitation and medical relief work was undertaken, and a number of workers came to Champaran who caused a real awakening among the peasants.

XI

Kaira Satyagraha

In the year 1918 there was a widespread failure of crops all over the Kaira District of Gujerat. According to the Land Revenue Code, in such conditions, if the value of the crop falls below a certain percentage of the normal, the cultivators can claim full suspension of the revenue assessment for that year. The farmers claimed that this condition was fulfilled, and applied for relief through the normal constitutional channels. Government, however, granted only partial relief and the distress being very great and further petitioning of no avail, Gandhi advised the farmers to offer Satyagraha and refuse to pay the tax. This they did. Government responded in the usual way. A few workers went to jail: property was confiscated. In the end an honourable peace was secured on Government promising that, if the well-to-do farmers paid up, the poorer people would be granted exemption.

Among the spiritual features of this Satyagraha, Gandhi notes that the peasants began to learn the new lesson of simplicity, and the new lesson of courage. The great difficulty was to preserve the spirit of courtesy when the old servility had disappeared. "Incivility spoils Satyagraha like a drop of arsenic in milk." Civility means not "the mere outward gentleness of speech cultivated for the occasion, but an inborn gentleness and desire to do the opponent good. These should show themselves in every act of a Satyagrahi."

This Satyagraha was not, to Gandhi's mind, perfect, for it did not leave the Satyagrahis stronger and more spirited than they were in the beginning. But it "marks the beginning of an awakening among the peasants of Gujerat, the beginning of their true political education."

XII

Rowlatt Acts Satyagraha

It was during the intense public indignation over the Rowlatt Acts that the principle of large-scale Satyagraha was first introduced in India. The Rowlatt Acts Satyagraha did not succeed of its object. It was called off after ten days. But it has two great achievements to its credit. It introduced the people of India to the idea, and gave them some hint of its mighty possibilities; and it offered to a nation thirsty for vengeance, eager for a violent revolution, a pacific solvent of its wrongs. Had not Mahatma Gandhi come forward just at that moment with his gospel of non-violence (I have been told) the Punjab would have flowed with rivers of blood. It was a spiritual miracle. A whole people was converted. That was the great victory of 1919.

The Movement commenced with an act of purification, a day of fasting and prayer. "Satyagraha," said Gandhi, "is a process of self-purification and ours is a sacred fight, and it seems to me to be in the fitness of things that it should be commenced with an act of self-purification." The day was observed in every part of India. It was a tremendous awakening. But the Movement which started with such high hopes came to a sudden end. The week that followed was rich in tragedy. The arrest of Gandhi and the deportation of Dr. Kichlew and Dr. Satyapal led to outbreaks of mob violence in Ahmedabad and Amritsar. There followed the terrible retaliation of Jallianwalla Bagh. But it was not the violence of the British that crushed Gandhi's spirit: it was the violence of his own followers. He saw that the way was not yet prepared. He confessed an Himalayan blunder. The Movement was suspended. The Mahatma fasted in deep humiliation and penance.

But the Rowlatt Acts Satyagraha was not a failure. It initiated that mighty adventure of national purification which is still in progress. It was the annunciation of the non-violent ideal. It emphasized the necessity of careful training and education in Satyagraha. It provided a convincing proof of the Mahatma's sincerity of purpose and his devotion to the spiritual ideal.

XIII

The Non-Co-operation Movement

The Report of the Hunter Commission, the debate in the House of Lords condoning General Dyer, and the violence done to Mussulman sentiments in regard to the Khilafat question caused the whole of India, in Gandhi's own words, to "lose faith in British justice and honour." Satyagraha was bound henceforth to take a new form, that of Non-Co-operation. Mahatma Gandhi wrote to the Viceroy in June 1920 explaining his own position. "The only course open to one like me is either in despair to sever all connection with British Rule, or, if I still retained the faith in the inherent superiority of the British Constitution to all others at present in vogue, to adopt such means as will rectify the wrong done." "Non-Co-operation was the only dignified and constitutional form of such direct action. For it is a right recognized from times immemorial of the subjects to refuse to assist the ruler who misrules."

The Satyagraha expressed in the form of Non-Co-operation was not an agitation designed to remedy some particular evil in an otherwise good Government, but it was a moral protest, a direct assault on a Government whose very foundations were considered to be evil.

Non-Co-operation Satyagraha was planned by Mahatma Gandhi to progress through four carefully graded stages, as it seemed that the country was prepared for them. The first was to give up all titles and honorary offices: the second was the withdrawal from the paid appointments of Government and a refusal to participate in any manner in the working of the existing machinery of the civil and judicial administration. The third stage was a no-tax campaign, and the fourth was to ask the police and the military to withdraw co-operation from the Government.

On August 1, 1920, Mahatma Gandhi inaugurated the Movement by returning his Kaiser-i-Hind gold medal to the Viceroy. The following month, the Calcutta Special Congress, after some vigorous controversy, adopted the famous Non-Co-operation resolution. This took Swaraj as the goal of the Indian people as the only way to vindicate the national honour. It was to be obtained by "a policy of progressive non-violent Non-Co-operation." The programme was outlined as follows: (*a*) The surrender of titles and honorary offices and resignations from nominated seats in local bodies; (*b*) Refusal to attend Government levees, Durbars, etc.; (*c*) Gradual withdrawal of children from schools and colleges owned, aided, or controlled by Government, and the establishment of national schools and colleges in their place; (*d*) Gradual boycott of British courts by lawyers and litigants and the establishment of private arbitration courts for the settlement of private disputes; (*e*) Refusal on the part of the military, clerical, and labouring classes to offer themselves as recruits for service in Mesopotamia; (*f*) Withdrawal by candidates of their candidature from the Reformed Councils and refusal on the part of the voters to vote for any candidate; and (*g*) Boycott of foreign goods. "And inasmuch as Non-Co-operation has been conceived as a measure of discipline and self-sacrifice (so ran the Resolution), the Congress advises the adoption of Swadeshi in piece-goods on a vast scale, and inasmuch as the existing mills of India with indigenous capital and control do not manufacture sufficient yarn and sufficient cloth for the requirements of the nation, and are not likely to do so for a long time to come, this Congress advises immediate stimulation of further manufacture on a large scale by means of reviving hand-spinning in every home and hand-weaving on the part of the millions of weavers who have abandoned their ancient and honourable calling for want of encouragement."

The Nagpur Congress of December reaffirmed this resolution and changed its creed to "the attainment of Swaraj by the people of India by peaceful and legitimate means." Henceforward, Mahatma Gandhi was to be the dominating voice in its affairs. Accompanied by the Ali brothers, he now toured the country, amid scenes of great enthusiasm. Many lawyers abandoned their practice: *panchayats* began to be organized: there was a great fall in revenue from stamps due to the decrease in the number of suits instituted in the law-courts. Thousands of college and school students were withdrawn from Government-controlled institutions. A National Muslim University was opened at Aligarh. Mahatma Gandhi inaugurated the Gujerat National University at Ahmedabad, a National College at Patna, and the Tilak Mahavidyalaya at Poona. The following year, thousands of students left their colleges at Calcutta and the Mahatma opened the Bengal National University. Not many honours and titles were resigned, but the Movement stripped such honours of their dignity. They were no longer coveted nor were their possessors admired. The spinning-wheel was widely popularized and there were many bonfires of foreign cloth. There was a spontaneous campaign against the liquor traffic with a corresponding fall in the Excise Revenue. Later, there came the great hartals on the occasions of the visits of the Duke of Connaught and the Prince of Wales—demonstrations which were in no way intended as insults to the persons concerned, but as an expression of protest against the refusal of Government to listen to the people's legitimate demands.

At first Government had ignored the Movement, regarding it—in Lord Chelmsford's words—as "the most foolish of all foolish schemes." By the end of 1920, however, a policy of repression was considered necessary, and a large number of volunteers went to prison. But it was not till after the boycott of the Prince's visit that the authorities became seriously alarmed, and that there were wholesale arrests of leaders and others. Even so, the repression, severe as it was even at this time, was as nothing compared with that which the country was to endure in 1930.

As yet, Civil Disobedience had not been offered. The Bezwada Congress Committee of March 1921 considered that the country was not yet ready for it. There were occasional outbreaks of violence which warned the leaders not to press forward too rapidly. In July the Committee again met in Bombay, and decided that Civil Disobedience should be postponed till after the completion of the Swadeshi programme, which was regarded as a test of the measure of influence attained by the Congress and the guarantee of the stability of the atmosphere of non-violence. It was not until the Ahmedabad Congress at the end of the year that Civil Disobedience was declared to be the only civilized and effective substitute for armed rebellion and local committees were authorized to organize individual and mass Civil Disobedience if they considered the people to be sufficiently trained in the ideals of non-violence. Mahatma Gandhi wrote to the Viceroy announcing his intention to inaugurate mass Civil Disobedience in Bardoli. But there followed the tragedy of Chauri Chaura, which Mahatma Gandhi took as a warning from God to change his plans, and the Civil Disobedience campaign was suspended. "We dare not enter the Kingdom of Liberty," said Gandhi, "with mere lip homage to Truth and Non-violence." A month later, he was himself arrested.

The calling off of the Movement was another of those acts of quixotic chivalry which are inseparable from Satyagraha. Satyagraha is a spiritual weapon, independent of external failure or success. The Satyagrahi can only be defeated through some failure in his own spirit. He can press forward to victory even through an apparent disaster. So it was in 1921. "Suspension of mass Civil Disobedience," wrote Gandhi at the time, "and subsidence of excitement are necessary for further progress; indeed, indispensable to prevent further retrogression. I hope, therefore, that by suspension every Congressman or woman will not only not feel disappointed, but he or she will feel relieved of the burden of unreality and of national sin.

"Let the opponent glory in our humiliation, or

so-called defeat. It is better to be charged with cowardice and weakness than to be guilty of our oath and sin against God. It is a million times better to appear untrue before the world than to be untrue to ourselves."

XIV

Bardoli Satyagraha

At the close of the historic struggle in Bardoli in 1928, Mrs. Sarojini Naidu wrote to Mahatma Gandhi:

"I have always felt and known that Satyagraha in its deep authentic sense is literally 'the treasure of the lowly'—Maeterlinck's beautiful phrase—of those who are content with realities and not seekers after false values and false standards. . . . Your dream was to make Bardoli the perfect example of Satyagraha. Bardoli has fulfilled itself in its own fashion interpreting and perfecting your dream."

The Bardoli Satyagraha arose over a dispute about the reassessment of the land-tax. According to the Land Revenue Code, this is reassessed every thirty years, and in 1926 a revision became necessary. On various grounds, most of which were disputed, the tax was raised 30 per cent. and over Rs. 150,000 extra above the normal tax was expected from the peasants. The storm of protest which greeted this demand resulted in the reduction of the required increment to 22 per cent., but this also the peasants felt to be greatly excessive. There is no room here to enter on the arguments advanced on either side: it will be sufficient to say that, as we shall see, Government ultimately admitted the substantial justice of the peasants' case. It goes without saying that before giving his support to the movement Mahatma Gandhi had to be assured that "the cause was just and the case unassailable."

Every possible attempt was made to obtain a settlement by constitutional means, and it was only after repeated failures that a Peasants' Conference passed a resolution to the effect that since in its opinion the revision settlement was arbitrary, unjust, and oppressive, they would refuse payment until an impartial tribunal was appointed to investigate or the enhancement was cancelled. The people of Bardoli were well prepared for Satyagraha. Many of Gandhi's Satyagrahis in South Africa were from this district. For years, his ashrams had been conducting social service work among the villagers. The chief points of his teaching were familiar to them. Above all, in Sardar Vallabhbhai Patel, they had a great peasant leader, one of themselves, whose cheery, virile, and heroic spirit had fallen under the spell of Mahatma Gandhi's Gospel of Non-violence.

There is no need to describe the campaign in detail. The peasants refused to pay, the Government was forced to retaliate. There were imprisonments, confiscations, the normal agonies of a subject race. The peasants resorted to locking themselves into their houses with their cattle, in order to escape the attachment of their property. The spiritual effects of Satyagraha were quickly manifested. The people were purified by suffering: they simplified their lives: they observed truth and non-violence with perfect loyalty. Sardar Vallabhbhai preached first fearlessness and then, as official repression grew, peace. "Our sacrifice has commenced, let it be pure and spotless. We have now only to offer ourselves as spotless, willing victims." The spirit of religion and of social purification was everywhere evident.

Bardoli became an all-India issue. Gandhi sternly forbade any kind of "sympathetic strike." If the peasants' cause was based on truth, it would prevail. And so it was. A truce was proclaimed; an official inquiry was appointed and, after exhaustive investigations, found that the peasants' complaints were substantially justified. The enhancement (for two Talukas) was reduced from Rs. 187,490 to Rs. 48,648 annually, a saving to the peasants of nearly one hundred and forty thousand rupees. The campaign had its effect in other provinces also. In the Punjab, lakhs of rupees were remitted from the tax and there were some liberal suspensions in the Central Provinces. The moral effect was even greater. Throughout the length and breadth of India the peasant gained a new dignity. The spirit of non-violence shown by Bardoli revealed to millions the possibilities of this new type of warfare.

The poet Rabindranath Tagore hailed the Bardoli Satyagraha as being full of the spirit of the Epic Age, a story of the triumph of moral right over arbitrary power through a fight in character unique in modern times.

XV

NEILL STATUE SATYAGRAHA

Towards the end of 1927, an agitation arose in Madras against a statue which had been erected in the middle of the last century to Colonel Neill, who was killed at the relief of Lucknow in the first Indian War of Independence, 1857. There seems to be no doubt, on British evidence alone, that Neill was a soldier of a peculiarly brutal type: there is no need to recall the tortures and indignities which he inflicted upon his Indian brothers, but it was more than enough to account for a strong feeling of indignation against a statue in his honour, bearing an eulogistic and quite inaccurate inscription.

A number of people in Madras, supported by the local Congress Committee, took the matter up, and offered Satyagraha. Some thirty volunteers were imprisoned. A motion in the Madras Legislative Council for the removal of the statue was defeated. Considerable public interest was aroused and Mahatma Gandhi blessed the movement in a number of articles in *Young India*. These are of great interest as giving us his views on the way such Satyagraha should be conducted.

"The Volunteers," he insisted, "must not be impatient. Impatience is a phase of violence. A Satyagrahi has nothing to do with victory. He is sure of it, but he has also to know that it comes from God. His is but to suffer."

Gandhi then makes a careful analysis of the

expenditure. He urges the utmost economy. "I would warn the Satyagrahis against spending much on meals, conveyances, and lights. . . . Strictest honesty and care are necessary in the handling of public funds. This is an indispensable condition of the growth of a healthy public life."

He criticizes a certain violence of language in the pamphlets issued by the Satyagrahis. "There is no room for the language of anger and hate." There was to be no enmity against the memory of Colonel Neill himself. "We seek to destroy the principle for which the statue stands. We wish to injure no man."

This Satyagraha was not, indeed, of outstanding importance and it was not successful, but we have referred to it because of the general principles which it illuminates.

XVI

Social Satyagraha

It must not be imagined that Satyagraha is a weapon that can only be used against a foreign Government. "Satyagraha," says Gandhi, "may be offered against parents, against one's wife or one's children, against rulers, against fellow-citizens, even against the whole world." There have been many examples in recent years of local Satyagraha, especially in connection with social reform.

An interesting instance of its use against a social evil was furnished in 1928 by some students in a Kaira village called Dharmaj. One of the citizens of the village proposed to give a caste dinner in connection with the twelfth-day ceremony of the death of his mother. A number of the more advanced younger people of the village, strongly disliking the custom, tried to stop the dinner. Failing in this, they took three vows:

1. Not to join their elders at the dinner or otherwise partake of the food served on that occasion.

2. To observe a fast on the day of the dinner as an emphatic protest against the practice.

3. To bear patiently and cheerfully any harsh treatment that might be accorded to them by their elders for taking this step.

And so on the night of the feast, a large number of students (some 285 of them) and even some children fasted. The older people were very angry and threatened them with various penalties. Mahatma Gandhi wrote congratulating the brave and spirited students on their action, assuring them that if they would persevere, all evil customs would be removed by the pure and beautiful weapon of love.

Not all such Satyagraha can be justified: those who would undertake it must be very sure of the justice and dignity of their cause and the ideals described in the earlier part of this chapter must be strictly followed. It is precisely here that the warnings of Mr. Jamshed Mehta, already quoted, must be carefully regarded. Education is necessary to prevent Satyagraha being offered for quite inadequate reasons or in the wrong spirit. At Dharmaj, however, the cause was just and all the conditions for a spiritual victory were observed.

Such cases of Satyagraha have recently become very frequent. In various parts of Gujerat and Kathiawar, the younger men and women are constantly turning this weapon against the holding of caste dinners after death, the marriages of young girls with old men, and several other evil social customs.

XVII

Satyagraha is rapidly becoming a powerful weapon in the hands of the "untouchables." Gandhi has claimed the noble figure of Nanda, the pariah saint of Chidambaram, as his forerunner in Satyagraha. Nanda, by prayerful perseverance, succeeded in gaining admission to the Temple which enshrined his Beloved. He had to pass through the fire and endure great suffering at the hands of the Brahmins, but won his way to victory, and is now enrolled among the threescore and three Shaivite saints of the Tamil Land. Gandhi said that when he heard of Nanda his head bowed before his spirit. "By his indomitable spirit and by his overwhelming faith in God, Nanda was able to bear down the haughty spirit of the Brahmins. . . . He broke down every barrier and won his way to freedom not by brag, not by bluster, but by the purest form of self-suffering. He did not swear against his persecutors; he would not condescend to ask his persecutors for what was his due. But he shamed them into doing justice by his lofty prayer, by the purity of his character, and if one may put it in human language, he compelled God Himself to descend and made Him open the eyes of the persecutors. . . . If many of us could possibly imitate Nanda and assimilate a spark of his spirit we can make this land a land again of holy people."

As though under the patronage of Saint Nanda, the first "untouchable" Satyagrahi, Gandhi inspired and directed a campaign in Travancore. A famous Hindu temple stands in the middle of the little village of Vaikom, at the meeting of four cross-roads. Since the houses along these roads are occupied by Brahmins, no "untouchable" is allowed to use them, although they are maintained from the public funds. A Christian follower of Mahatma Gandhi determined to challenge this rule, and taking an "untouchable" in his company, walked quietly down the road. He and his companion were beaten by the Brahmins. They came again and were arrested by the police. A great many others then followed and were also arrested. At last the authorities erected barriers across the road. Then the Satyagrahis sat daily for many weeks before the barriers in an attitude of prayer. Many occupied themselves in spinning. So deeply did this action touch the public conscience that a few Brahmin lawyers threw in their lot with the "untouchables." When the monsoon burst upon the country, the roads were flooded, but the Satyagrahis kept their place. Gandhi exhorted them to carry on "without fatigue, without despair, without anger, or irritation, and with forbearance towards their opponents and the Government." Their actions were to be marked by gentleness, the utmost, humility, uniform courtesy

At last their self-suffering had its reward. The roads were opened, and opened not only in Vaikom, but all over Travancore.

Similar Satyagraha has been offered more recently in Poona, at the famous Parvati Temple, at Munshiganj (where—owing to the efforts of high-caste women—it was successful) and at Nasik. At Nasik, a large crowd of "untouchables" under the leadership of Dr. Ambedkar (a delegate to the Round Table Conference), demanded entry to one of the Hindu temples. Batches of Satyagrahis sat before the closed gates all day long, chanting the Holy Name of God. Everyone was struck by their perfect non-violence and discipline. An aged Brahmin was deeply moved by what he saw, and emptied his purse into the hands of an "untouchable" Satyagrahi, saying that such devotion could melt the stone walls of the temple but not the hard heart of orthodoxy. Unhappily, the hard heart or orthodoxy remains unmelted at both Nasik and Poona.

But in spite of such set-backs as these, Satyagraha has put a most powerful instrument in the hands of the people. Its triumph carries a message of hope to all subject races and all depressed communities. It carries a challenge to the strong nations also, that they may be noble enough to use this weapon of the great. It may yet prove to be the one antidote, not only of war, but to a violent communist revolution like that of Lenin. For Satyagraha is the potential remedy of capitalism no less than of war. "A successful Satyagraha," says Gregg, "will prove far more potent against capitalism than any violent or communist struggle has been or could be. It will modify trade unionism profoundly." Love is actually the most potent revolutionary force in the entire world. Gandhi has been much criticized for not making a direct frontal attack on the great capitalists. He is not their enemy, it is said, but their friend. The truth is that his principle of Satyagraha contains so much spiritual explosive that he can trust it to do its own work. He is the friend of all men, coolie and millionaire alike, that in all he may effect a change of heart. When that change of heart is accomplished, whether it be in the shrines of endowed orthodoxy, in the offices of great magnates, or in the war councils of the nations, it will be a victory not only for India, but for the moral forces of the whole world.

XVIII

Civil Disobedience of 1930–1931

We are at present too close to the Civil Disobedience Movement of 1930–1931 to write its history, the main outline of which will be familiar to all our readers. In this book we are concerned primarily with the moral issues that underlie public events: and therefore we will confine ourselves to asking in what way the Movement of 1930 illustrates the great moral principles of Satyagraha.

In the first place, the year 1930 exhibited the utility of Satyagraha as a possible substitute for war in international relations. If ever a country has been eager and ready for war, it has been India in the last two decades. Mahatma Gandhi fully realized the dangers of Civil Disobedience. "It is undoubtedly fraught with great dangers and difficulties," he told the *New York World* in January 1930, "but infinitely less so than the present danger of unbridled but secret violence breaking out in many parts in India, owing to understandable and pardonable impatience on the part of many youths." During 1930, the principle of Satyagraha was put to a supreme proof. The non-violence of the people was tested to the uttermost. Their leaders were arrested, and there were no great figures to lead them. The whole machinery of the Government was brought to bear upon the Movement. Every form of propaganda was utilized to suppress it. Yet in spite of the embarrassment caused to the Satyagrahis by the sporadic attempts at violence made by the Revolutionary Party, the nation as a whole, bereft of leaders, its organizations declared illegal and dispersed, its press muzzled or destroyed, kept loyal to the principles of Truth and Non-Violence, and thus made its way to victory. India showed that Satyagraha was not only practicable but could be carried to success. The success of a Satyagraha campaign is, of course, entirely dissimilar to the vulgar triumph of a violent war. It does not aim at the humiliation or destruction of the enemy: it desires rather to leave him ennobled and purified. Such was the issue of 1930 Satyagraha, and such was the kind of unvictorious-victory of the Gandhi-Irwin pact.

The real victory was far greater than any local

or national success. Sardar Vallabhbhai Patel, in his Presidential Address at the Karachi Congress at the end of March 1931 declared, "Thanks be to God that the awakening was a call to self-purification. Though there have been aberrations, it is a fact beyond challenge that India has given a singular proof to the world that mass non-violence is no longer the idle dream of the visionary, or a mere human longing. It is a solid fact capable of infinite possibilities for a humanity which is groaning for want of faith beneath the weight of violence, of which it has almost made a fetish. The greatest proof that our Movement was non-violent lies in the fact that the peasants falsified the fears of our worst sceptics. They were described as very difficult to organize for non-violent action, and it is they who stood the test with a bravery and an endurance that was beyond all expectation."

A new hope has dawned upon the world as a result of India's bloodless war of freedom. Gandhi has said, "If India's self-consciousness rises to the height necessary to give her a non-violent victory in her fight for freedom, the world values will have changed and most of the paraphernalia of war will be found to be useless."

In the second place, the Movement of 1930 well illustrates the many forms which Satyagraha can assume. The Mahatma himself tended to concentrate on the breach of the salt-laws, that is to say, on what he regarded as an immoral system of taxation which he felt it was his duty to destroy. A large number of his followers took up the boycott of foreign goods, especially of foreign cloth, in order to give some protection and support to Indian industries. The vigour with which this was carried on may be seen from the fact that in one month (September 1930) the monthly imports of piece-goods dropped from 160 million yards in the corresponding month of the previous year to 48 million yards in 1930. The import of foreign cigarettes fell in that month from thirteen lakhs to two. Even more effective was the peaceful picketing of liquor shops and opium-dens, which was made illegal by Ordinance. A number of distinguished men and a great army of minor officials resigned their posts. Later there was a widespread movement to refuse co-operation with the Census officials. Special forms of Satyagraha were made possible by the promulgation of Ordinances. All Congress organizations were declared illegal, and many leaders went to prison for maintaining their membership. The Press Ordinance, which made the publication and sale of unauthorized news sheets unlawful, was widely challenged. A pamphlet addressed to the military by the Congress was distributed and led to many arrests.

In Gujerat and the United Provinces a No-Tax-Campaign was vigorously prosecuted. In the United Provinces this was based on economic needs and aimed at economic betterment: in Gujerat the Movement was primarily political. In Bihar the Chaukidari tax was withheld and parts of the province suffered greatly from the imposition of a punitive police force and the confiscation of property. In the Central Provinces and elsewhere, "Forest

Satyagraha" (that is breach of the Forest Laws, which many felt to be too burdensome), was successfully carried on.

Everywhere, by means of processions, public meetings, hartals, flag-salutations, etc., the will of the people found vigorous and unmistakable expression.

It is important to notice what the object of the Campaign really was. It did not aim at embarrassing the Government by cutting off its supplies. It did not desire to impoverish workers in Lancashire for the benefit of workers in India. The leaders never wished for a discriminatory boycott of *British* goods: they wished to protect Indian industries and therefore tried to boycott all foreign goods. The resignation of officials was not intended to make the administration impossible, but to protest against it. These things were sometimes forgotten by the supporters of the Movement, and generally misunderstood by its opponents. The principle of Satyagraha, however, is quite clear. In his evidence before the Hunter Committee in 1919, Mahatma Gandhi was asked, "Is not the underlying idea embarrassment of Government?" to which he replied, "Certainly not. A Satyagrahi relies not upon embarrassment but upon self-suffering for securing relief." The presence in the Gandhi-Irwin pact of a clause aimed at stopping the boycott of British goods was due to the fact that the ideals of the leaders had not been properly interpreted, and that there was a tendency to such discrimination among the rank-and-file of the Movement. Such an attitude was, however, entirely contrary to the principle of Satyagraha and to the wishes of the leaders. In the third place, we should note that while the Campaign as a whole was the expression of the desires of the entire nation, it was led by a compact, well-disciplined and highly organized army of volunteers. For their guidance the following rules were laid down, and for the most part implicitly obeyed.

RULES FOR A SATYAGRAHI

As an Individual

1. A Satyagrahi, i.e. a civil resister, will harbour no anger.
2. He will suffer the anger of the opponent.
3. In so doing he will put up with assaults from the opponent, and never retaliate; but he will not submit out of fear of punishment or the like to any order given in anger.
4. When any person in authority seeks to arrest a civil resister, he will voluntarily submit to the arrest, and he will not resist the attachment or removal of his own property, if any, when it is sought to be confiscated by the authorities.
5. If a civil resister has any property in his possession as a trustee, he will refuse to surrender it, even though in defending it he might lose his life. He will, however, never retaliate.
6. Non-retaliation excludes swearing and cursing.
7. Therefore a civil resister will never insult his opponent, and therefore also not take part in many of the newly coined cries which are contrary to the spirit of *ahimsa*.
8. A civil resister will not salute the Union Jack, nor will he insult it or officials, English or Indian.
9. In the course of the struggle if anyone insults an official, or commits an assault upon him, a civil resister will protect such official or officials from the insult or attack even at the risk of his life.

As a Prisoner

10. As a prisoner, a civil resister will behave courteously toward prison officials, and will observe all such discipline of the prison as is not contrary to self-respect; as, for instance, whilst he will *Salaam* officials in the usual manner, he will not perform any humiliating gyrations and he will refuse to shout "Victory to Sarkar" or the like. He will take cleanly cooked and cleanly served food, which is not contrary to his religion, and will refuse to take food insultingly served or served in unclean vessels.
11. A civil resister will make no distinction between an ordinary prisoner and himself, will in no way regard himself superior to the rest, nor will he ask for any conveniences that may not be necessary for keeping his body in good health and condition. He is entitled to ask for such conveniences as may be required for his physical or spiritual well-being.
12. A civil resister may not fast for want of conveniences whose deprivation does not involve any injury to his self-respect.

As a Unit

13. A civil resister will joyfully obey all the orders issued by the leader of the corps, whether they please him or not.
14. He will carry out orders in the first instance even though they appear to him insulting, inimical, or foolish, and then appeal to higher authority. He is free before joining to determine the fitness of the corps to satisfy him, but after he has joined it, it becomes a duty to submit to its discipline, irksome or otherwise. If the sum total of the energy of the corps appears to a member to be improper or immoral he has a right to sever his connection, but being within it, he has no right to commit a breach of its discipline.

15. No civil resister is to expect maintenance for his dependents. It would be an accident if any such provision is made. A civil resister entrusts his dependents to the care of God. Even in ordinary warfare wherein hundreds and thousands give themselves up to it, they are able to make no previous provision. How much more, then, should such be the case in Satyagraha. It is the universal experience that in such times hardly anybody is left to starve.

In Communal Fights

16. No civil resister will intentionally become a cause of communal quarrels.
17. In the event of any such outbreak, he will not take sides, but he will assist only that party which is demonstrably in the right. Being a Hindu he will be generous towards Mussalmans and others, and will sacrifice himself in the attempt to save non-Hindus from a Hindu attack. And if the attack is from the other side, he will not participate in any retaliation but will give his life in protecting Hindus.
18. He will, to the best of his ability, avoid every occasion that may give rise to communal quarrels.
19. If there is a procession of Satyagrahis they will do nothing that would wound the religious susceptibilities of any community, and they will not take part in any other processions that are likely to wound such susceptibilities.

Fourthly, we need to remember that the Movement of 1930 was no mere struggle for the transference of political power. It had a moral foundation. It was a campaign to restore that national self-respect and honour without which a lofty morality is not possible. It aimed at regaining the fullness of life which for generations had been impaired. It wanted freedom for reform and progress, which every nation can only accomplish for itself. Above all, as we have seen in another chapter, it was concerned about the poor. The chief burden of Gandhi's indictment of British rule in his Letter to the Viceroy was that Britain had taxed and impoverished the poor of India. The terrific pressure of the land revenue, the heartless impartiality of the incidence of the Salt Tax, the drink and drug revenue, all fall most heavily upon the poor; while "if the weight of taxation has crushed the poor from above, the destruction of the central supplementary industry, i.e. hand-spinning, has undermined their capacity for producing wealth."

"The British rule," said Mahatma Gandhi, "has impoverished the dumb millions by a system of progressive exploitation and by the ruinously expensive military and civil administration which the country can never afford. It has reduced us politically to serfdom. It has sapped the foundations of our culture and by the policy of disarmament it has degraded us spiritually. Lacking inward strength, we have been reduced by all but universal disarmament to a state bordering on cowardly helplessness."

It was thus the sense of spiritual and moral impoverishment that drove Mahatma Gandhi into opposition. It is important to stress this, for Satyagraha is too pure and holy a weapon to be exploited by self-seeking politicians. Gandhi and his lieutenants had an absolute faith in the justice of their cause.

On the eve of the March which initiated the Satyagraha Campaign of 1930, the Mahatma declared before a vast audience on the sands of Sabar mati: "I have faith in the righteousness of our cause and the purity of our weapons. And where the means are clean, there God is undoubtedly present with His blessings. And where these three combine, there defeat is an impossibility. A Satyagrahi, whether free or incarcerated, is ever victorious. He is vanquished only when he forsakes truth and non-violence and turns a deaf ear to the Inner Voice. If, therefore, there is such a thing as defeat for even a Satyagrahi, he alone is the cause of it. God bless you all and keep off all obstacles from the path in the struggle that begins to-morrow. Let this be our prayer."

It was in this spirit that the campaign was carried on. We have already described the social reform movement which accompanied it. "I am positive," said Gandhi at the beginning of National Week (that week which wrought so profound a change in the national consciousness of India), "that the greater the dedication to the country's cause and the greater the purification, the speedier will be the glorious end for which the millions of India consciously or unconsciously are striving."

Rabindranath Tagore has recently pointed out that he found that the attention of the West had been attracted to India not only by her struggle for political freedom, but by the inherent moral appeal of the methods she is pursuing in the attainment of her object. "India," he said, "has created a new technique in the history of revolution, which is in keeping with the spiritual traditions of our country, and if maintained in its purity will become a true gift of our people to civilization."

In the fifth place, there can be no doubt that the entire nation was ennobled and purified through the patient enduring of great suffering. You may find bitterness and hatred in the houses of the rich whose fortunes have been imperilled; you may find it in the hearts of those who have stood aloof from the struggle, but you would not have found it in the gloomy overcrowded prisons, or in the wards of the Congress Hospitals. I will give two personal examples. I shall never forget a visit I paid to Sabarmati Jail to see Mahadev Desai, Gandhi's devoted secretary and disciple. It was like going to a place of pilgrimage. Such great love and generosity radiated from my friend in his convict's garb, that I came away uplifted and ennobled.

I remember talking to a boy—he was not more than 19—in the Congress Hospital in Bombay. He had gone to Sholapur simply to offer National Flag Satyagraha, by hoisting the flag and taking the consequences. On arrival he had at once been arrested with his companions, all of them unarmed, defenceless boys; they were each put in separate cells, stripped naked, brutally assaulted in the most delicate parts of their bodies, and flogged till they fell senseless. My friend had been in hospital six weeks and was still suffering. But what amazed me was, not the amount of his suffering, but the quality of his love. There was not a word of bitterness or anger. He was a Satyagrahi and it was his duty to suffer that he and thus his motherland might be the purer.

We have no desire at this stage to recall the

sufferings inflicted by the authorities on the people at Peshawar, Bombay, Borsad, indeed all over India in 1930. It was the duty of Christian missionaries to have made eloquent protest in the name of humanity and justice at the time. It came as a moral shock to many non-Christians, and it stands to the lasting discredit of the Church in India, that such protest was not made. Even in the Visitors' Book of the Congress Hospital in Bombay, only one missionary society is represented. That, however, is now a thing of the past. There is no advantage in perpetuating an unhappy memory. But we must refer to the sufferings of the people, not in order to condemn the police, but to praise the wonderful spirit of patience and endurance shown by their victims.

The non-violence of the Satyagrahis exhibited the violence of the authorities not as a thing to be accepted as natural and inevitable, but as in itself an evil and hateful thing, a method which must be rejected by mankind. Satyagraha has always the widest possible reference: it attacks not only a particular kind of evil, but all evil: it has assailed not only the British domination in India but the very idea of military force on which that domination is founded.

In fact, as the Mahatma anticipated, the sufferings of the people were enough to melt the stoniest hearts. The fact that it was necessary to imprison the noblest and purest leaders of the nation awoke deep concern in all liberal and generous-minded Englishmen. World-opinion, and especially opinion in America and parts of Europe, became strongly sympathetic to the Indian cause. There must be something to be said for the claims of a people who are willing to suffer so much for them. The very remarkable change to be observed in the outlook of countless English people to-day is not only due to the speeches of the delegates to the Round Table Conference, or to the making of trouble in India, but above all to the spiritual effect that real and universal suffering must have upon all good men. Here again, the Civil Disobedience Movement was an appeal to conscience, and as such, it did not fail in its aim.

Finally, we must notice the remarkable moral effects of the Movement. "Whether we agree with the policies and methods of Mahatma Gandhi or not," says Mr. C. R. Reddy, "there can be no disagreeing with the fact that, so far as the national character is concerned, he has done more to strengthen and elevate it than all the Indian universities put together."

During the last year India has become a new country. The non-violent war of Satyagraha has evoked chivalry, devotion, loyalty on a scale unparalleled. A well-known missionary remarked to me last year, "This Movement is perfectly exhilarating; unlike a war of violence, it draws out all the best in people." The very hope of freedom has freed the *souls* of millions. The peasants, who for centuries have had no vision beyond "their loves or else their sheep," have found some great ideal to live for. The dull soul of the merchant has been lifted by the thought of sacrifice: the ambition of the lawyer has turned to a new channel; the religion of the religious has won a new note of service, the service of the Motherland.

Here is a wealthy girl who abandons her silks for the simplest homespun, restricts her diet, and prays morning and evening after the example of the Mahatma. There is a young student who has fallen under the spell of the new moral idea. Once he was wasting his manhood and betraying his honour, to-day his life is disciplined as a monk's: for any irregularity he observes a fast: in clothes, food, sleep and recreation he is carefully restrained. One day he brought me his arm-chair, for no disciple of Gandhi could use such a thing. Here is a Mohammedan motor-driver who, two years ago, was a notorious drunkard. To-day he is living a temperate life, and runs a night-school for illiterate Mohammedans in his town. Or again, there is a wealthy merchant living almost with the simplicity of a peasant. You may see members of the noblest families of India dressed in the plain white khadi which has nothing to distinguish them from their poorer brothers. To a man like Sardar Vallabhbhai Patel, the message of Gandhi brought a new note of earnestness into public life. "I was a dandy and wasted all my time out of court in playing bridge. I was sick of the politics of the day, which to me were a byword for poltroonery and hypocrisy. At that time came Gandhi. He opened my eyes and showed the way. His earnestness and seriousness captured me and I was a changed man."

This earnestness and seriousness has infected the other national leaders, and a new public morality, founded on Truth and Service, is growing up in India. Gandhi himself says that, from 1920, Indian public life has been dominated by the idea that "since truth and non-violence were the sole means to be employed by the Congress to reach its goal, self-purification was necessary even in political life." "The very essence of our civilization is that we give a paramount place to morality in all our affairs, public or private."

It is no easy matter to proclaim Truth in a country where the press is muzzled and where secrecy is an almost essential foundation of prestige, or to stand for Non-Violence against a Government that rests on force for its very existence. In no way is Gandhi more at variance with the world than in this battle of ideas. If they can be carried over into the Swaraj Government of the future, there is a great hope for the world. It is more than possible that this may be so, for to Gandhi and his followers the struggle for Swaraj is a spiritual struggle. He once told a Burmese audience in Rangoon, "My friends, if you will become torch-bearers lighting the path of a weary world towards the goal of ahimsa, there is no other way out of it, save that of self-purification and penance."

XIX

The Salt Raids

A special feature of the Salt-Tax Satyagraha and one which greatly puzzled many of the most deeply "pacifist" supporters of Mahatma Gandhi, was his policy of conducting raids on the salt depots at Wadala, Dharasana and elsewhere in May 1930. It is very difficult to understand how such raids could be reconciled with the strict creed of non-violence. But it is clear that Gandhi did not find anything inconsistent, and we must therefore try to understand his mind in the matter.

To those who feel that the Raids represented a form of aggression and were violent at least in effect, I fancy he would reply that Satyagraha is not the same as Passive Resistance. They differ "as the North Pole from the South." Satyagraha is entirely consistent with direct action. Gandhi claims both Christ and Buddha as his exemplars in this respect. "Buddha fearlessly carried the war into the enemy's camp and brought down on its knees an arrogant priesthood. Christ drove out the money-changers from the temple of Jerusalem and drew down curses from heaven upon the hypocrites and the Pharisees. Both were for intense direct action. But even as Buddha and Christ chastised they showed unmistakable gentleness and love behind every act of theirs."

The Salt Laws are regarded by Mahatma Gandhi and his followers as so anti-social and iniquitous that some drastic form of protest was necessary to overthrow them. Professor J. C. Kumarrappa has clearly stated the case against the Salt Tax.

The Salt Tax is the worst blot on our revenue system. In a vegetarian country like ours a greater amount of salt is needed in the diet; and in a tropical country a greater quantity is used in the household for preserving various articles from putrefying. What is more, the poorer people whose menu varies very little from day to day require a good deal more than the upper and the middle classes. We know that the rest of our tax system bears heavily on the poor and this is the last straw to break the camel's back. If the people had all they needed, the consumption of salt should be inelastic, but the wide variation in demand with every change in duty imposed clearly indicates that the tax makes the people stint on this most essential article of diet. In India a tax on salt is almost as bad as a tax on good drinking water. This tax itself is highly regressive both actually and relatively. The poorer the citizen the more he pays, and a larger share of his income is taken than from the richer man. In the sober words of the Taxation Inquiry Committee, "it falls on a necessary of life, and to the extent that salt is essential for physical existence, it is in the nature of a poll tax. The bulk of it is paid by those who are least able to contribute anything towards the State expenditure. Salt is also required for various industrial and agricultural operations and for cattle. Unless it is issued free for these purposes, some burden is thrown upon the industries in which it is used." Even a meat-eating country like England abolished the duty on salt over a hundred years ago. Japan, which received a revenue of about 10 million yen from the salt monopoly, abolished it in 1919 in consideration of "social policies"; it is ordinarily sold there now at almost cost and for agriculture, fisheries, etc., at even below cost.

But it is not only avowed Nationalists who have held this opinion. Mr. Ramsay MacDonald himself has declared the Salt Tax to be "an exaction and oppression," and many other administrators have wished to see it abolished.

Mahatma Gandhi, therefore, considered that he and his followers had an inherent moral right not only to make salt, but also to take possession of the salt in the depots where it was awaiting distribution. There was no question of "theft." The volunteers were ready to pay the keepers of the depots for the salt they removed. The point was that the salt, not yet having been distributed, had not yet been taxed; the volunteers were ready to pay the natural price of the salt but not the enormous and unnatural increment (2,400 per cent. on sale price!) of the tax. It was felt that the Raids would illustrate in a vivid and convincing manner the absurdity of the tax, and thus help towards its abolition.

The Raids were also a protest against the methods which the police had been adopting in dealing with the Satyagrahis. In his letter to the Viceroy explaining the reasons for the steps he intended to take, Gandhi made it quite clear, first that he regarded it as his natural human right to take possession of the Government salt-works, and secondly that he was doing so because in his opinion Government was not meeting the Satyagrahis in a civilized manner. "I could have had nothing to say if in dealing with the civil resisters the Government had satisfied itself with applying the ordinary processes of law. Instead, while the known leaders have been dealt with more or less according to the legal formalities, the rank-and-file have been often savagely and in some cases even indecently assaulted. . . . Before then the reign of terrorism that has just begun overwhelms India, I feel that I must take a bolder step, and if possible divert your wrath in a cleaner if more drastic channel.

. . . For according to the science of Satyagraha, the greater the repression and lawlessness on the part of the authority, the greater should be the suffering courted by the victims. Success is the certain result of suffering of the extremest character voluntarily undergone." The Raids to Gandhi represented an adventure in suffering: it is certain that he never associated them with violence. In the same letter, he reiterates his creed, "The only way to conquer violence is through non-violence, pure and undefiled."

The Raids were, in fact, a direct appeal to conscience. "An Englishman," said Mahatma Gandhi once to Mr. C. F. Andrews, "never respects you till you stand up to him. Then he begins to like you. He is afraid of nothing physical; but he is very mortally afraid of his own conscience, if ever you appeal to it and show him to be in the wrong." The Raids were a drastic attempt to show the British Government that in two respects—in the Salt Tax and in the use of force—it was in the wrong.

From this standpoint, the Raids may be said to have been successful. The Satyagrahis were unable to capture any salt, but they captured the sympathy and imagination of the world. Even those who hoped that such a method would not be repeated could not withhold their sympathies from the broken and tortured volunteers. Their sufferings gave the Salt Tax a prominence which it could have gained by no amount of agitation. The treatment given to the Satyagrahis was such as to discredit the armed forces of any Government. One of the leaders on his arrest at Dharasana said, "I do not think we have been defeated because we have not been able to get a pinch of salt at Dharasana. There is no defeat in a Satyagraha campaign. The greater the amount of sacrifice the greater the success. I do believe that the sacrifice and suffering at Dharasana must have, in smaller or larger measure, softened the hearts of officers, military and policemen. The constant flow of sacrifice on the field of Dharasana and elsewhere shall continue and it shall either mend this Government or end it."

XX

Looking back over the ideals of Satyagraha and their varying embodiment, can we claim that we have here the much sought and longed-for "Moral Equivalent for War"? An equivalent we must have: we cannot simply abolish war. "Any real programme of peace," says Walter Lippmann, "must rest on the premise that there will be causes of dispute as long as we can foresee that these disputes have to be decided and that a way of deciding them must be found which is not war." Moreover, war represents certain positive values which must be preserved: we could not abolish war without impoverishing mankind. Our substitute for war must preserve these values. William James, in his famous essay, *A Moral Equivalent for War*, says that these values are fidelity, cohesiveness, tenacity, heroism, conscience, education, inventiveness, economy, and physical health and vigour. H. G. Wells, in *First and Last Things*, has also written on this subject. He says that war embodies the great ideals of order, discipline, the ideal of service and devotion, a high standard of physical fitness, the sense of responsibility. Walter Lippmann in an article on *The Political Equivalent of War*, says, "It is not sufficient to propose an equivalent for the military virtues. It is even more important to work out an equivalent for the military methods and objectives. For the institution of war is not merely an expression of the military spirit. It is not a mere release of certain subjective impulses clamouring for expression. It is also—and I think primarily—one of the ways by which great human decisions are made. If that is true, then the abolition of war depends primarily upon inventing and organizing other ways of deciding those issues which have hitherto been decided by war."

We believe that in Satyagraha such a way has been discovered. We believe that from the practical standpoint alone, Satyagraha can be as effective as war, and that from the moral standpoint it immeasurably transcends it. We believe that Satyagraha embodies all those higher values whose preservation is desirable. We have already described the moral effect of the National Movement in India; much of this is the direct result of Satyagraha. The Satyagrahis have exhibited magnificent courage, of a far higher order than the excited and passionate bravery of the battlefield. They have maintained a high ideal of discipline and order. They are dominated by the thought of service. Their devotion has been put to the supreme test of unpaid labour. With the constant arrest of their leaders, the sense of responsibility has been aroused, and every Satyagrahi has become a potential leader. In this form of warfare you cannot keep your general staff in safety behind the lines: the mortality, in fact, is greater among the Generals than in the rank-and-file. The capacity of inventiveness is developed through the necessity of constantly devising new ways of offering Satyagraha. In a movement of self-purification, economy, truth and conscience are leading factors of success. Satyagraha has now been proved to be one of the ways in which great human decisions have been achieved.

Richard Gregg gives eight points in which Satyagraha resembles war.

1. In having a psychological and moral aim and effect.
2. In principles of strategy.
3. In a discipline of a parallel emotion and instinct.
4. As a method of settling great disputes and conflicts.
5. In operating against the morale of the opponents.
6. In requiring courage, dynamic energy, capacity to endure fatigue and suffering, self-sacrifice, self-control, chivalry, action.
7. In being positive and powerful.
8. In affording opportunity of service for a large idea and for glory.

But Satyagraha possesses these qualities in a purer and nobler fashion. The most obvious advantage of Satyagraha over war is that it reduces the number of casualties, replaces falsehood by truth, and expects to gain its end not through the possession of superior force, but through the justice of its cause. But it has other advantages not so obvious.

Satyagraha, unlike war, does not demoralize the combatants. Rather it ennobles those on both sides. I am ready to believe that the police who conducted lathi-charges in Bombay are better men to-day than they were a year ago. Their victims certainly are. I have stayed in some of the "War Camps" of Gujerat: I could not help comparing them with the camps described in *All Quiet on the Western Front*. On the one side, frantic hysteria, nerves stretched to the breaking point: on the other, calm and lofty equipoise. There was drunken valour: here valorous temperance. There was foul language and sordid ideas: here was the very spirit of religion. In Europe, men were being degraded to the level of beasts: in India they were being raised to the highest levels of which humanity is capable.

Satyagraha has all the romance and adventurousness of war. It has the element of risk, and not a few are called to lay down their lives. It is, I think, a nobler bravery, a bravery of the soul, to which the Satyagrahi is called.

It is economical: it does not involve a huge outlay in weapons, barracks, pensions. It is a warfare of ascetics, fit child of a nation which is pre-eminently the mother of ascetics. It is an expression of the democratic spirit; it bestows no titles, no decorations; it does away with all class-distinctions. Its warriors may be recruited from every walk of life and it is specially suited to women, and even children can play their part. Its possibilities are infinite: there is no situation in which it cannot be applied.

It is "an all-sided sword; it can be used anyhow; it blesses him who uses it and him against whom it is used. Without drawing a drop of blood, it produces far-reaching results. It never rusts and cannot be stolen."

CHAPTER IV

THE PLACE OF THE CHRISTIAN CHURCH IN THE NEW INDIA

There can be little reasonable doubt that the success of India's long struggle is in sight, and more violent methods alone have been successful in India. Whether we like it or not, whether we view the prospect with anxious fears or with those high hopes which I have urged should take the place of fears, we shall within the course of the next few years see an India which, whatever may be her precise relation to Great Britain, will be as free to control her own affairs as the other free countries of the world. Some attempt must now be made, in conclusion, to show the part which the Christian Church may play in this new India, if it rises to the height of its opportunities. I will try first to indicate briefly something of what I conceive that part to be, and then discuss at greater length the conditions upon which its fulfilment of that part depends.

I believe, then, that the Christian Church in India, in spite of its smallness, might well fulfil an important rôle in the shaping of the India that is to be. In "the Christian Church in India" I include Indian Christians, who will form increasingly the vast majority; Anglo-Indians, who (it is greatly to be hoped) will more and more find their truest opportunities of development and usefulness as a community in throwing in their lot with the land of their birth; and foreign Christians, who will be a small and diminishing number, but still able to serve the Church in India, if they will, for some years to come.

I

Opportunities of Service of the Christian Church

(1) India will have a right to look to the Christian community to give valuable help in the maintenance of a high moral standard in India's public life.

It is essential, for instance, for the future well-being of the country, that a strong tradition of integrity and incorruptibility in the public services should be built up. The fears frequently expressed that in a free India this tradition will be lacking must be shown to be groundless. The Christian community must take its full share in the public life of the country and, together with other communities, provide for the public services men of tried moral worth, known to be proof against bribery and corruption.

Further, it will be necessary that the different communities should lay aside communal claims and privileges and throw themselves into the task of building up a united nation. Here it is open to Christians to set a good example. Of recent years a number of the leaders of the Christian community have earned the gratitude of the country by the way in which they have urged that community not to stand for special communal advantages, but to throw themselves into the national cause, asking only such recognition as their actual services might merit. This attitude of the Christian leaders has won widespread recognition. Mr. N. C. Kelkar, the Poona Nationalist leader, at a large public meeting paid a fine tribute to it. Pandit Motilal Nehru, whose untimely death has caused such universal sorrow, when asked why they did not mention the Christians when talking of communal issues, said that "they did not mean to disregard the Indian Christian, but the reason why they did not mention him when talking about communal issues is that the Indian Christian community is the only community that is not a problem to the country, for they are the only ones taking the right attitude in reference to this matter."

It must be admitted that such tributes have not always been entirely deserved, and that the Christian community as a whole has not yet responded fully to the appeal of its leaders; but, if they will do so, they will give a fine example for the other minority communities to follow.

In general it may be said that the progress of the new India will depend largely on the degree in which it secures the help in its public life of men and women imbued with the spirit of self-sacrificing service; and surely those who profess to follow One Who came to be the servant of mankind and sacrificed His life for this end should be able to supply a high proportion of such devoted and self-forgetting patriots.

One such example of a great Indian Christian

patriot is fresh in our minds. Mr. K. T. Paul, whose early death is a grievous loss not only to the Indian Christian community but to India as a whole, was amongst the first to show how important a part Indian Christian leaders could play in the public life of their country, and to inspire his fellow-Christians with the spirit of national service. An indefatigable worker, he laboured day and night for his country's moral, social, and spiritual uplift, and it was his unsparing devotion to his labours at the Round Table Conference in the cold of an English winter which eventually hastened his end.

His services have won notable tributes from every side. Of these I will quote one,—that of the Hindu editor of the *Indian Social Reformer*.

While devoting his powers to the service of the Christian movement in India, Mr. Paul was a strong and enlightened Indian nationalist. In 1930 he resigned his position as National Secretary of the Y.M.C.A., anticipating by a year the retirement age, in order to serve the country in the political sphere. He has always opposed communal representation, holding that the Christian community should throw in its lot with the main body of the citizens, and when he stood for election to the Madras Legislative Council he therefore chose to contest a university seat rather than to stand for election by the Christian community. Mr. Paul served his apprenticeship at Salem on the municipal council and on the district board. He was closely identified with the Co-operative Movement and in 1927 served on the Committee on Co-operation appointed by the Government of Madras, as also in 1920 on the Fraser Commission on Village Education. He was therefore peculiarly fitted, both by his intimate knowledge of Indian problems and by his international contacts, to accept the invitation of the Viceroy to be one of the two Christian representatives at

> the Round Table Conference. In London he made a valuable contribution to the deliberations of that council, but hardly less valuable was his work as a public speaker, his many contacts with the Christian Churches giving him a unique opportunity of explaining the Indian point of view to English audiences.
>
> Mr.Paul was an indefatigable worker, and spent himself without stint in serving the causes he had at heart. . . .
>
> A devout Christian, Mr. Paul was deeply attached to the culture and traditions of his ancestral faith and worked in terms of close co-operation with his countrymen of all creeds and classes.
>
> He was a man of deep family affections and a warm friend. He would have played a leading part in the nation-building activities of self-governing India, had his life been spared for some years more.

There is every hope that the next twenty years will show many Indian Christians of the calibre of K. T. Paul, playing their part in the building of the new India.

(2) Further, India may well look to the Christian community to help in the work of reconciliation and peace-making between the different races and religions of the country.

There can be no doubt that the task of adjusting the respective claims and interests of the many diverse elements which go to make up the Indian nation will be one that for many years to come will test the constructive abilities of Indian statesmanship in a high degree. In the case of many of the issues which will come up for settlement Christians, by the neutral position which they occupy, will have special opportunities for fulfilling the rôle of arbitrators or peace-makers; and in a free India their help will be welcomed in a measure which was not possible under the old regime, when their association in men's minds with the ruling power inevitably caused their intervention to be regarded at times with some suspicion.

(3) But the principal contribution which the country has a right to expect that Christians will make to the new India is in the application to public and private life of the principles of Christ and their exemplification in Christ-like character. It is possible that efforts may be made to suppress aggressive propaganda aimed at winning converts to the Christian Church, though the recent "declaration of rights" issued by the Congress states that all people will be given the right to profess and practise their religion without hindrance[1]; but, in any case, it is certain that, unless the present Indian outlook becomes radically altered, nothing but welcome will be extended to all efforts directed at making the teaching of Christ more widely known and followed; and no task confronting the Christian Church in India will compare in importance with that of trying, both by the written and spoken word, and by the still more eloquent witness of Christ-like conduct, to permeate the national life with the spirit and the principles of Jesus Christ. This is, of course, a task incumbent not only, or mainly, on foreign missionaries, who will be a rapidly decreasing number, but on those Christians whose home is India,—a task parallel to that

[1] This matter is more fully discussed in the closing section of this chapter.

which English Christians have to perform for England, and which is needed at least as urgently in England as in India. It is a task which, properly understood, is free from the spirit of proselytizing which Christ so severely condemns. It is not the desire to win as many adherents as possible, by whatsoever means, to the ranks of the Christian community. It is rather the desire to share with others the Church's supreme treasure, which is Christ. The passionate enthusiasm which has ever animated the ambassadors of the Cross, and which is inseparable from all vital Christianity, has its true spring in the love of Christ Himself and the knowledge of His preciousness. His apostles are men who "count all things as loss for the excellency of the knowledge of Christ Jesus," their Lord, and who could not, if they would, be guilty of the utter selfishness of refusing to share with others the secret which has transformed their own lives with joy and power. They must needs "witness" of Christ; and such witness, borne with no compulsion other than that of love transparently sincere, will never alienate the best minds, nor ultimately fail of its purpose.

Here, then, are some of the ways in which the Christian Church should play its part in the new India. In all this I am not attempting to claim for the Christian community any superior moral excellence over other communities. I am only too sadly conscious of our failure even to approximate to the Christian standard. My object has been simply to indicate some of the ideals which Christians might well place before themselves at this critical epoch; and we have now to consider the essential conditions on which the fulfilment of these ideals depends.

II

Conditions Necessary for the Church's Effective Service

(1) The first essential condition for the Church's effective service in the new India is the disappearance of racial superiority on the part of the foreigner and the overcoming of all racial barriers.

If the Christian Church can show that it possesses the secret of true brotherhood it will bear most effective witness for Christ. Christ Himself said, "By this shall all men know that ye are My disciples, if ye have love one to another"; and He prayed that the world might have convincing evidence of His divine mission in the supernatural unity of all who should believe in Him.

We know that, in the early days of the Church's history, this did actually happen. One of the most self-authenticating evidences to the Roman world of the truth of the Christian claims was the new spirit of brotherhood prevailing among the followers of Christ,—a brotherhood holding in its equal embrace the cultured Greek and the unlettered "barbarian," the proud Roman and the exclusive Jew, the slave-owner and his slave. A religion which could do this bore on it manifestly the hall-mark of its divine origin. A like impression would be made in India to-day if Christians there could show a like brotherhood. India is searching for the secret of unity. There is no greater enemy of her progress than communal and religious dissension. She would welcome with open arms any who could show her plainly and indisputably the secret by which this could be overcome. The Christian Church would be able to bear most powerful witness to the truth of her claims and to the Master whom she professes to follow, if she were seen to be a true international brotherhood, acting uncompromisingly on the principle that in Christ there is "no Jew or Greek; barbarian, Scythian; bond or free," but in Him all are one. Unhappily, it cannot be said that this principle has yet been fully accepted by the Church in India; for racial discrimination is still even too painfully apparent.

We must, indeed, recognize with thankfulness that in India Christians of different races worship together quite commonly in the same churches. It is, of course, natural that, on account of language difficulties, Indians and Europeans should, in general, have separate services; but it is quite common to find a considerable number of Indian worshippers at an English service attended mainly by Europeans or Anglo-Indians, and a few English or Anglo-Indians in a congregation predominantly Indian.[1]

[1] It is rare to find occasions such as happened once on my boat going to England, when the three Indian Christians with me were refused Communion, and (needless to say) I had to refuse to receive without them.

But in the matter of religious ministrations the position is still far from satisfactory. I am afraid it must be said that, in spite of a few welcome exceptions, the ministrations of Indian clergy are not acceptable to English or Anglo-Indian congregations. It is, of course, quite legitimate that a congregation (whether English or Indian) should desire to have, in permanent charge, one who belongs to the same race and shares the same traditions as the predominant number of its own membership; but one could wish that English congregations might be more eager to have occasional ministrations from Indian clergy as a witness to the fact that the Christian Church is an inter-racial brotherhood. The fact is that, while the ministrations of English clergy are welcomed by Indian congregations, and it is still not uncommon for an Englishman even to be in charge, the appearance of an Indian at the altar or in the pulpit of an English church, even though he may have a perfect command of the English language, is so widely resented that it seldom happens; and many English church people would refuse to receive Communion from Indian hands. In one case an English congregation, deprived for a time through illness of the services of its chaplain, refused the proffered ministrations even of the English priests of a brotherhood whose members live in Indian style and are known to be sympathetic towards Indian nationalism.

It must also be confessed with sorrow that the social relationships between English and Indian Christians still leave much to be desired. I would far rather omit mention of this, but if we are to envisage fairly what the new day requires of us, it is necessary to face up to our own failings. I think of a missionary receiving a joint call from three Englishmen and an Indian, and inviting the Englishmen into his house while he left the Indian outside till the others insisted on his being brought in. I think of another missionary pitching a little tent in his compound for two guests, one Indian and one English, because (as he said) "I never have Indians in my house." I think of a large bungalow in which a number of devoted missionary ladies live together, but where no Indian fellow-worker can ever be invited to a meal because some of the inmates object. These instances and others like them, for which I can vouch, relating not to nominal English Christians but to those who are giving their lives to the work of propagating the Gospel, sound, I know, almost incredible to Christians in England; but there is a subtle poison of racial superiority, emanating inevitably from the atmosphere that our racial dominance has spread around us in India, which has extraordinary power of corrupting even most self-sacrificing servants of Christ. A young missionary coming out from England with no sense of racial arrogance, desiring only to serve India in the spirit of Christ, instead of mixing from the first freely with the people of the country, gets largely isolated from them in an English household, and unless he be a person of exceptionally strong character, becomes slowly and unconsciously infected with the prevailing outlook.

I have no desire to exaggerate this social estrangement of the races. There are, of course, a large and increasing number of instances of most happy Christian fellowship between Indians and English, in which no such disparity is felt. But I am afraid it remains true, on an impartial review of the whole situation, that these instances must be regarded as the exceptions, and that, in the vast majority of cases, the Indian Christian regards his fellow English Christian as one separated from him by a subtle consciousness of superiority,—one whom he may respect as a good man but not love as a brother. And too often this induces in the Indian Christian an "inferiority complex," which makes him oversensitive to supposed insults, and in any case cripples his full self-expression and usefulness for the service of the Church and nation. Here, then, is an essential task devolving on those from the West. In the new India all racial barriers in the Church must be boldly overthrown. "The middle wall of partition" must be seen openly as taken away by Christ. Not only must Christians of different race worship freely together, but English congregations must, from time to time, welcome the ministrations of Indians; and in places where (as will be increasingly the case) there are no clergy of their own race to minister to them, the English residents must be glad to rank themselves as members of the local Indian congregation.

In our social relationships with Indian Christians (as with all Indians) we of the West must resolve to do away, once and for all, with our "superiority complex," our patronizing, our aloofness, and be content to be, quite simply, brothers and friends. The missionary, in particular, must realize that inability to overcome "colour prejudice"—always a fatal hindrance to useful work—must debar him from work in the new India altogether. Further, every missionary coming to India from the West should, normally, spend his first year or two at least in an Indian household, where he will not only pick up the language far more efficiently than by attending "Language Schools," but will also imbibe naturally the Indian "atmosphere" and the Indian point of view, will become acquainted with the manners and customs, the etiquette and conventions of the country, and in a word will become a naturalized citizen of India, able to move freely and courteously among the people of the land, recognized by them at once as one of themselves rather than one who, with the best will in the world, remains strange and *gauche* and difficult of approach in Indian society. The sooner such intimate association with Indians begins, the better. Dr. S. Jesudason, a greatly respected Indian Christian, writes:

> A would-be missionary should seek to form intimate, personal friendships with Indian students resident for purposes of study in his country, not in the spirit of patronizing condescension, but on terms of mutual helpfulness and heart-felt love. Failing this, he should, as soon as possible after his coming to this country, place himself under the leadership and guidance of an Indian or Indians who command his confidence and respectful love. He should scrupulously avoid being led away by his own countrymen, especially in his attitude towards Indians or things Indian.

He must have his eyes ever open to study the Indian mind and adapt himself or completely change any preconceived views as he seeks to form these intimate personal friendships. His purely Western angle of vision as regards life and its value may have to change completely."

There are some amongst us whom Christ calls to an even closer self-identification with the people of India, amounting to an abandonment of our own national ways and customs to a great extent, and an adoption of those of India. I do not suggest that all missionaries are called to this. But I believe that *all* are called to become one in spirit and outlook with those whom they seek to serve, and that many would find they could do far more profitable service, particularly in an India freed from Western control, if they would frankly adopt the ways of life of the country. To quote Dr. Jesudason again:

A missionary who comes to this country must cease to be in truth a member of his own nation. If God calls him to come to India it is because He wants him to become one of our people. Otherwise why should he leave his own country and people to go and serve a foreign nation? This complete identification with the people whom we seek to serve is the very fundamental principle of love behind the incarnation of Jesus Christ. Mere outward profession of accepting the principle will not do. India is shrewd to detect pious frauds. He should feel India as his home and not the country he has left, and completely identify himself with the people of the land in their aspirations.

It is sometimes urged that such adoption of Indian manners by Westerners only gives offence to Indians, savouring to them of unreality and pose. The answer to this is that, if there is no inward sympathy of spirit answering to the outward change, it will indeed give an impression of hypocrisy and cause offence. But I have never known Indians do otherwise than welcome the adoption by Englishmen of the dress and ways of life of the country, where this is associated with an inward self-identification with the Indian outlook. The very fact that we of the West regard it as quite natural for an Indian to adopt English ways and dress in England, but strange for an Englishman to adopt Indian customs in India, is really an unconscious sign of our racial superiority. When India stands on the same footing with us as a free country, it may become the normal thing for the English in India to do as India does; and such an attitude, if adopted, will certainly have beneficent results. More than this, it is to be hoped that many missionaries and others will of their own choice become "naturalized" as Indians by law, and so throw in their lot completely with India as their adopted country.

But, however this may be, the racial superiority of the Western Christian must go; as it goes, the "inferiority complex" which it has bred in the Indian Christian will go too. English and Indians will begin to understand and to love one another as brothers in the one family of Christ; and the Church will begin once again to bear witness by love and unity to its divine Lord.

(2) A second necessary condition of the Indian Church playing its full part in the new India is that it should have the same freedom as we hope will

now be accorded to the Indian nation. It would be lamentable indeed if the Churches of the West were to prove more slow and timid than the State in the bestowal of real independence instead of rather leading the way in bringing to an end all that savours of foreign domination.

What influence, in an India which has secured Swaraj, could possibly be exercised by a Church still under Western tutelage? Could Hindu and Moslem citizens of a free India look with any respect to a Christian Church directed mainly by foreigners? And yet that will be the condition of affairs unless either a revolution takes place in the mentality of missionaries and missionary societies, or the Indian Church breaks violently away from the West. The second alternative—that of a complete alienation of the Indian Church from the Christians of the West—would be most lamentable; but at the moment, in some parts of the country at least, there is imminent danger of its occurring.

It is, however, the former alternative that we must all desire. What is really needed is that *"missions" and "missionaries," as such, should now come to an end, being merged in the Indian Church.*

There are a few instances in which this has already taken place. The outstanding example is that of the Syrian Christian Church in Travancore, which for centuries has been an autonomous Church, entirely independent of the West, and ruled by its own Indian bishops.[1] Another district which (thanks

[1] The Jacobite Syrian Church is, indeed, under the Patriarch of Antioch, but this is quite a different matter from the missionary control of which I am speaking.

largely to the courage and foresight of Bishop Whitehead in getting a young Indian appointed Bishop as long ago as 1913) is now approximating to the same condition is the Anglican Diocese of Dornakal. The missionaries here are a small and diminishing number, and are partly under the direction of the Diocese. The pastoral and evangelistic work of the Church is almost entirely in Indian hands. The result is most striking and noteworthy. The Indian clergy of the Diocese are a most keen and inspiring body. At a recent week of retreat and conference for them which I attended, all but three or four (who were reasonably prevented) out of a total of a hundred were present, though attendance was entirely voluntary, and one could not but be impressed by their fine spirit. The Diocese has witnessed one of the most striking "mass movements" into the Christian Church in all India, and one largely free from the defects too often associated with such movements. The evangelistic work being in the control of Indians who are not in a position to offer temporal advantages to the converts, the dangers arising from the attractions of material benefits are largely eliminated.[1] Moreover, every communicant of the Church before his Confirmation has been personally examined by the Bishop, and the sincerity of his convictions tested. Thus the acceptance of Christianity has meant a moral

[1] I do not mean by this to imply that Western missionaries deliberately "bribe" people to become Christians, but that the advantages of education or status which their position enables them to offer to Christians are apt to encourage motives lower than the best.

revolution in the lives of the depressed classes in this Telugu area, and so striking and manifest has been this moral uplift of the outcaste that the caste people, as a result, are following suit, and coming in great numbers into the Christian Church. The large financial contributions to the work of the Church made by the converts, whether of caste or outcaste origin, are a further witness to the reality of their Christian convictions.

Other instances of the Indian Church possessing real autonomy could also be cited, and during recent years there has been a notable advance in many of the missions in the direction of transferring responsibility to Indian hands.

But, in spite of this, it remains true that, in the main, missionaries still control the affairs of the Indian Church. In the subordinate posts a good deal of independent authority is in Indian hands; but in the last resort the decision on all matters of importance rests with the missionary body. I think it will hardly be denied that this is still the normal position. One disastrous result of this situation is that comparatively few of the ablest and keenest young Indian Christians are coming forward for ordination. Men of independent character and initiative shrink from entering the ministry when they know that (in the great majority of cases) they will have to serve under a foreign missionary society, and be under the direction of the local missionary in charge. Their reluctance is still further increased when they know that (again in the great majority of cases) their salary will be a quarter or a third, or at the most half, of that of the missionary, and their whole manner of life correspondingly more straitened than his.[1]

We must, indeed, recognize with thankfulness that it has become quite common of late, in the more progressive missions, to give some prominent Indian in the ministry the title of "missionary" and a status and salary approximating to that of Western missionaries. But something far more drastic than this is now required. Now that India as a whole is to have a real control of her own affairs, and the British yoke is to be removed from off her shoulders, the Indian Church must at the same time be made really autonomous. "Missions" and "missionaries," as such, must (as I have said) come to an end. They must be swallowed up in the Indian Church. Whilst missionary societies must obviously be faithful to such contracts as they have already entered into with those now in the field, all those coming out in future will, if the changes I envisage take place, be on a new footing. Men and women from the West, ready to come out in the spirit of service and not wishing for leadership, will still be welcomed by the Indian Church, as they will by the Indian nation. They will sit with the Indian Christians on the Church Councils, and will equally with them be under its direction. They will

[1] For the sake of those unfamiliar with Indian conditions it may be stated that a Government chaplain draws a salary of about Rs. 1,250 and a missionary about Rs. 250–500. A *few* Indian clergy get salaries like Rs. 150 or 200, or even more. The great majority get about Rs. 60–100, and some even as little as Rs. 20 or 30.

not possess special privileges or advantages merely on account of their race. They will be on exactly the same footing as Indians who possess similar qualifications. The spectacle (now common) of a raw recruit from England being placed over the head of men who have grown grey in the service of the Church must once and for all come to an end.

I am convinced that the best type of young Englishman proposing to devote his life to the work of Christ in India would far rather offer his services to the Indian Church than to a missionary society. I have abundant evidence for saying that this is so even now. Still more will it be so when India has Swaraj. Just as there will be Englishmen, and those of the finest moral calibre, ready to go out and serve the Indian nation, if she desires their help, upon whatever terms India herself may think right, so, still more, will there be keen Christian men and women eager to serve the Indian Church under whatever conditions that Church may lay down. They will feel that to go to India as emissaries of a foreign missionary society would give them an unnatural and intolerable position.

It will be said that, as the missionary societies provide the salaries, they must also control the missionaries whom they send. But is this necessary? Must he who pays the piper always call the tune, even in the affairs of the Church? The S.P.G. has always acted on the principle of handing over a "block grant" to dioceses abroad, leaving the mode of its expenditure (apart from the salaries of missionaries) to be determined by the Bishop (in consultation, presumably, with his Diocesan Council). Why should not all societies do the same? And why should not this principle be now carried to its logical conclusion by bringing the missionaries under the block grant on the same terms as other workers, viz. that their salaries, pensions, and conditions of service should be determined not by the foreign society, but by the Church into which they come.[1] No doubt the missionary would be taking a certain risk in thus submitting himself to the control of the Indian Church, but is the ambassador of Christ to shrink from risks? Any risk is worth while which would bring to an end the missionary's present position of superior isolation and safe privilege, and make him one with his Indian brethren. And I am confident that a foreigner, thus identifying himself with the Indian Church, would seldom have cause to complain of ungenerous treatment.

I submit, then, that unless the Church of the West is going to fall disastrously behind the whole movement of the times in regard to India, it must at once drastically revise its mission policy. We have reached the point at which "missions" must be willing to die in order to live, to be lost in the Church that they may be found in fruitful service.

When Mr. John R. Mott founded the interdenominational councils in India some twenty years ago, they were "missionary councils" and did a useful

[1] The Indian Church would naturally seek the help of the societies in the selection of new men or women coming out from the West, in so far as it still requires such.

work in bringing missionaries together; but Indian Christians, save for a few of the elect, were conspicuous by their absence.

A decade past, and after the visit of Mr. J. H. Oldham, the councils were turned into "Christian Councils," in which half the membership is nominated by the "missions" and half by the "Church."

Now, after nearly another decade, the time has come when "mission" nomination should vanish, and the Church councils in every place should nominate all the members of these central bodies, sending to them Indian or English delegates as they will.

Similarly, the first stage of the Christian enterprise in India was that in which, necessarily, missionaries held practically all the control in their own hands, while associating a few leading Indian Christians with them.

The second stage has been that in which the Indian Church has learnt to play its part side by side with the "missions," which have continued to exist as independent entities, both Church and mission being often conscious of strain and tension between them, but still working together on the whole with reasonable harmony.

The third and final stage, which we must now enter, is that in which the Indian Church, having served her tutelage, enters on her full autonomy, and is mistress in her own house. She will not bar the doors to those from another land who desire to come in a spirit of service and help her in her great task of evangelism. Nay, rather, she will give them generous and eager welcome as her guests. But she will look to them to show the courtesy of the true guest, who never usurps a place that is not his, and never outstays his welcome.

On the eve of his departure from India Lord Irwin received a letter, signed by over one hundred of the non-official Europeans of Bombay, the first part of which ran as follows:

> SIR,—We, the signatories of this letter, are all members of the younger generation of non-official Europeans in Bombay.
>
> Some of us may have twenty and even thirty years of service to India before us. To us falls the duty of co-operating with Indians in the building up of a new India. We shall live in an atmosphere foreign to that in which the older generation of Europeans have done their work.
>
> With the views of the older European generation, you, Sir, must be very familiar. The older generation has the advantage of greater experience and longer residence in this country. Yet few of the older Europeans will remain here to establish contacts with the new India. The Europeans who are soon to offer the helping hand are men like ourselves —men who have not yet reached the age of thirty-six. We are, therefore, encouraged to address this letter to you.
>
> For we believe that the burden which your patient statecraft places upon our shoulders is one which no adventurous Englishman would wish to cast down.
>
> Whatever seeming loss there may be in privilege and prestige, there is no loss whatever in the opportunities of individual service and personal influence. You have shown us that there are no obstacles that a statesman endowed with courage, good sense, and imagination cannot surmount; and you have quickened the spirit of good will and mutual trust that were but lately in jeopardy.

If that is the spirit animating the younger Europeans

in the service of the State, how much more will the Church of the West be able to send to India men willing to abandon "privilege and prestige" in order that in humility and love they may serve India and Christ.

Before leaving the question of the Indian Church's autonomy, a word ought perhaps to be added on the necessity of its being free, not only from mission control, but also from all interference on the part of Government. Whether the Government be predominantly British or predominantly Indian in character, it must exercise no control in the internal affairs of the Church.

"The Church of India, Burma and Ceylon," which till March 1930 (under the title "The Church of England in India") was a part of the established Church of England, is the Church which stands in most danger in this respect. In spite of the fact that by the Church of India Act it has now become a free Church, Government seems hardly to have realized this change; and there have been a number of instances lately in which Government has tried to control the action of missionaries and other members of the Church, not only by direct representations (which they are fully entitled to make), but indirectly by pressure brought to bear on the Bishops as Government officials.

Moreover, the fact that the Government chaplains are priests of the Church of India, Burma and Ceylon produces a somewhat anomalous and difficult situation. In a good many cases the Bishop himself will receive the salary of a Government chaplain for his ministrations to the troops; the Archdeacon of the Diocese will be a Government chaplain; and a number of such chaplains will sit on the Diocesan Council. So long as this is the case, the Church can hardly escape the charge of being still to some extent a Church under Government control; nor can it have full freedom for self-development along Indian lines. Moreover these chaplains and their lay representatives in the Councils will find it tedious to sit on assemblies where the great bulk of the business will increasingly be concerned with the affairs of the Indian congregations.

I believe that the right solution of this difficulty is that the Government chaplains should in future be frankly military chaplains, coming out with the troops, and attached to the Church of England rather than the Church of India. The objection that this would rob the Church of parish priests, or that it would divide the Church on racial lines, is met by the fact that Europeans outside the Army, and the Anglo-Indians and domiciled communities, would still be ministered to by other chaplains who would sit on the councils of the Indian Church, so that the witness to inter-racial unity would be preserved, and the needs of the civil population met. The military chaplains, on the other hand, would be recognized as being only birds of passage, attached to the steadily diminishing British Army, with no permanent stake in the country. The separation of this military element from the Church of India, Burma and Ceylon would leave the latter untrammelled in providing for the needs of the permanent residents of the country, and would also, incidentally, remove the ground of some of the charges most commonly levelled against that Church from the Indian side, e.g. of having amongst its clergy highly paid Government officials; of displaying Union Jacks and regimental colours in its churches; and of seeking to immortalize in its memorials, not only the courage of great men which all would desire to honour, but also many incidents which still rankle in Indian hearts and which in the new days of co-operation are best consigned to oblivion.

It need only be added that, if a Swaraj Government were to make any attempt to restrict the religious liberty of the Christian Church, or to impose its own authority upon it, it would need to be resisted with the same determination as that with which any such attempt by the present Government is to be opposed.

(3) A third necessary condition of effective work and witness by the Christian Church in the new India is that it should throw itself yet more fully into the national life.

Less than a generation ago it used commonly to be charged against Indian Christians that they had allowed themselves to become denationalized, that they contributed little to political life, and that, in so far as they were concerned with it, they tended to support the foreign bureaucracy rather than the cause of the nation.

Of late years, thanks to the emergence of leaders like Dr. Datta, K. T. Paul and Joseph Baptista, the position has considerably altered; and it is now generally recognized that the Christian community is rapidly awaking to the claims of national service, and is supplying a body of useful workers in the national cause—men who, in various walks of public life, are making a valuable contribution to the country's progress. The emergence of a "Christian Nationalist Party" in Bombay during last year is a characteristic sign of the times.

But more is needed. The number of Christians who are known as helping forward the public life of the country is still few. There is still too much tendency to regard religion as an affair of the individual soul, and to ignore the larger obligations which it imposes. I think it is true that Indian Christians still need to develop a keen social consciousness. What is required is something parallel to the movement of "Christian Socialism" associated with the names of Frederick Denison Maurice, Charles Kingsley and Henry Scott Holland in England in the last century—a movement which will claim for religion life in all its departments and in its widest scope, a movement which will see the redemption of society to be no less the end of religion than the redemption of the individual. As this conception—which is rapidly taking hold upon Indian Christian students—becomes dominant in the Christian Church as a whole, we may expect to see Christians coming forward in far larger numbers in the various avenues of public service.

As, side by side with this, devotion to India as the Motherland becomes more and more a powerful motive in Indian Christian hearts, we may expect to see the call of that Motherland for the best service of her sons and daughters widely heard and answered by members of the Christian community, as by those of the other communities of the land.

(4) A further condition of useful service is that the Indian Church should conserve and value all that is best in the social, cultural and spiritual heritage of the country.

If Indian Christians in the past have been looked on with a certain suspicion and disfavour on the ground that they failed to share in the national aspirations and efforts, and sided rather with the foreign masters of the country, it has similarly, and even more commonly, been charged against them that they have forsaken the social and cultural traditions of their ancestors and adopted the customs and ways of life of the West, thus alienating themselves from the mass of their fellow-countrymen.

A good many things might be urged in answer to this charge, as, for example, that the enormous majority of Indian Christians are those who live in the villages and are by no means Westernized; or again, that the great bulk of converts to Christianity are drawn from those classes which Hinduism has largely excluded from its "social and cultural heritage," and therefore they cannot be said to have forsaken it; or, once more, that large numbers of people belonging to other communities besides the Christian have developed the customs of the West.

Nevertheless, there remains a sufficient measure of truth in this charge of denationalization, at least as directed against educated Indian Christians of the past generation. And it has to be confessed that, even still, Hindus do feel that Indian Christians are separated from them by a good many quite needless barriers, having nothing to do with differences of religion. The dress, the food, the household arrangements, the manner of life of many Christian families are such that the Hindu, unless he has himself adopted Western customs, finds it hard to be at home amongst them. It would not be courteous or desirable for a foreigner to attempt to offer advice in these matters of social customs which every family or group must settle for themselves. I would, therefore, only express my joy at noticing that there is even in the cities an increasing number of Indian Christian households, in which Western customs are being replaced by those of the country, and my hope that this tendency may grow, so that there may be no hindrances to the freest social intercourse between Christians and those of other communities.

The Christian Church must, also, not be behind those of other faiths in appreciation of India's splendid literary heritage. Here we have, it must be confessed, been open to grave reproach. It is comparatively rare to find among us scholars really familiar with the great Sanskrit classics, or even with the treasures contained in the literature of the various vernaculars. In some parts of the country (owing largely to the inadequate and literal translations of the Bible and other books made by missionaries who have not properly grasped the language) Christians have developed a language of their own, marked by curious solecisms of grammar and idiom.

In this matter, once again, improvement is taking place. A real development of interest in good literature is evident within the Christian Church; conferences are held with the object of promoting a higher literary standard among Christians; and a number of young Christian authors are coming forward able to appeal by their writings to the educated community as a whole.

But it is India's *spiritual* heritage which is the richest of all. Indeed, the great bulk of her literary heritage is religious in character. There is an amazing wealth of religious ideas, a vast store of religious experience, enshrined in the sacred books of the Hindus.

Is the Christian Church to scorn all this wealth—to declare that she has nothing to learn from these monumental labours of the Hindu sages, that she can gain nothing by the study of the Hindu Scriptures? Such an attitude would certainly be contrary to the best traditions of the Christian Church itself. The Church made free use of Greek philosophical ideas and terms in building its own edifice of doctrine. The tenets of Neo-Platonism were carried over into Christian mysticism. The works of Aristotle were employed with almost sacred reverence by the schoolmen.

If the Christian Church is to commend its teachings to India, it can only do so by clothing them in the ideas and language which India understands.

What a wealth of material is to be found, for instance, in the *bhakti* literature, for expounding the principles of Christian devotion! How splendid a basis for treatises on Christian ascetic theology is provided by the system of Yoga!

But I would go farther. We turn to the Hindu Scriptures, not only to find language by which to interpret Christian teaching to India, but to enrich our own conception of the Christian teachings themselves. We may often find fresh light thrown on truths with which in an inadequate measure we have been long familiar by the study of Patanjali or the Gita, of Dnyaneshwar or Tukaram. God has nowhere left Himself "without witness"; and the truths which He has revealed to the heart of India should be precious above all to Christians, believing as they do, with St. John, that the Divine Logos "lighteth every man." They will find Christ re-interpreted and more deeply understood, as they study the way in which, "in diverse parts and in diverse manners," that Logos illumined the sages of India; and they will learn more clearly how Christ comes "not to destroy, but to fulfil."

Christian worship provides one of the opportunities for making use of this spiritual heritage of India. We already read in our churches the whole of the Jewish Scriptures, many passages of which are admittedly below the standard of Christ's own teaching, and indeed quite deliberately overpassed by Him. Why should not we choose many of the exalted passages from the Hindu religious books (the "first old Testament" for India, as Narayan

Vaman Tilak called them) for reading in the same way? In the literatures of the various vernaculars there are large numbers of hymns most suitable for Christian use, and Dr. A. J. Appaswamy has done good service for the Christian community in bringing together a number of such in his collection called *Temple Bells*.

In our regular teaching, as well as in our worship, we can also make rich use of the Hindu Scriptures. In particular, all students in our divinity schools and theological colleges should be made acquainted with the finest of these Scriptures, not with a view to showing how they may be refuted or condemned, but with a view to appreciating the national heritage into which they enter.

Towards the close of the second century A.D. there sprang up in Alexandria the famous Catechetical School, founded by Pantænus, who himself became a missionary to India, and made illustrious by the labours of Clement and Origen, whose teaching exercised an enormous influence over the thought of their own and later times. One of the outstanding marks of this teaching, as is well known, was the breadth of its outlook towards other religions and particularly towards Greek philosophy. The stress laid by them on the Jehannine teaching of the Divine Logos enables them to speak of Socrates as "a Christian before Christ," and to see in all the wisdom of the ancient world rays emanating from the one divine sun of Truth.

There is a quite remarkably close parallel between the Roman Empire of the second century and the India of to-day, from the point of view of the task confronting the Christian Church; and the next twenty years may well witness in India the establishment of a Catechetical School similar to that of Alexandria, in which Christian teachers, thoroughly versed in the Hindu Scriptures and revering them as part of God's utterances to men, will, with their aid, expound the great doctrines and principles of the Christian faith, and show Christ to India in such wise that India shall recognize Him as her own, and lay at His feet the homage of her richest *bhakti*.

If Indian Christians will, in these and other ways, show that they love and value, no less than others, the great cultural and spiritual heritage of their country, then only can they hope that their own distinctive contribution as Christians will be appreciated at its true worth.

(5) For, lastly, the Indian Church can only hope to render its own characteristic service to India if it is wholly and unflinchingly true to the teaching and the spirit of Christ Himself.

When Mahatma Gandhi was asked by Dr. Stanley Jones whether he desired to send through him any message to the people of America, he replied that he would urge them to teach and practise the *whole* of their religion, without diluting it or explaining it away.

This, after all, is our essential task. However desirable it may be that we should, as I have urged, seek to appreciate and use the spiritual treasures of Hinduism, Hindus will always continue to have a fuller understanding of these than Christians possess, and will be the natural expounders and interpreters of them. What India will ask from us Christians is that we be interpreters of Christ.

And, as Mahatmaji has said, we must set forth the whole truth of Christ without glossing over those elements in it which human nature, for one reason or another, finds hard of acceptance. Christians can never be eclectics, choosing what appeals to them and rejecting what they dislike, making their own individual judgment or fancy the test of what they will hold. Christ is their Truth, His teaching their standard—a thing wholly objective and concrete.

But the manner in which, both for teaching and life, Christ is for Christians central and final, means that there is always a likelihood of their appearing arrogant and exclusive. In stressing the finality of Christ, they appear to be setting themselves up against others. In maintaining that all men need Him, and in seeking to bring all men to the knowledge of Him, they appear to be guilty of a narrow-minded intolerance. This appearance is perhaps inevitable—inherent in the very *universality* of the Christian claim, which has always aroused opposition and dislike. Stephen, the first Christian martyr, was put to death for asserting it. Most of the later martyrs suffered in the same course. "Evangelism," the proclamation of good tidings for all mankind, is of the essence of the Christian religion.

Nevertheless, we do well to bear in mind that if

arrogance and intolerance become a reality, and not simply an appearance, in the conduct of Christians, they are being untrue to the spirit of Christ. In the true Christian there is no place for these things. Arrogance! Why, the Christian is pledged to utter humility by his following of the "meek and lowly" Christ. Like Paul he counts himself the chief of sinners, "not meet to be called an apostle." Only by the grace of God, showered upon him through Christ, is he what he is. But then, if Christ can work such wonders as to bring light and healing even to such a worthless creature as himself, what can He not do for others, for all men! And so out of his very humility, out of his consciousness of utter futility, springs his passion to proclaim the wonder of Christ! "Woe is unto me if I preach not the Gospel!"

There is here, if rightly viewed, no arrogance. Nor should there be any intolerance. Intolerance is the spirit which is unable to bear those who differ from it, which must force them by hook or by crook to agree or else be swept away. Nothing could be more alien to the mind of Christ than this. His way (with the significant exception of His final attempt to cut through the hard hide of bigotry and pride in the Pharisees by one slashing denunciation) was always the way of quiet persuasion, of loving appeal to the reason and conscience. And His followers can know no other way. Any thought of compulsion in drawing others to Christ must be to them utterly repugnant as well as futile. Any impatience with one who holds a different creed, any contempt of him or sense of superior excellence, should be wholly impossible. The true Christian will count all men better than himself. He will love all men, whatever their creed or convictions. He will rejoice in full unfettered friendships with men of other faiths, welcoming the friendship for its own sake and not as a "bait" for the friend's conversion. He will seek, never for a moment to lord it over others, but only and everywhere, like his Master, to serve.

Only he can never forget, if he be indeed a friend of Christ, that the one supreme service he can render any man is to share with him his own unique treasure. He has gained the treasure through no merit of his own. He has discovered it by the guiding hand of God. It has enriched his life beyond all imagining, so that the world's whole aspect is now for him transformed. He longs, out of a heart of selfless love, to impart to all who will receive it this treasure, which grows richer the more it is shared. There is no intolerance or arrogance, but only humble and loving loyalty, in being thus true to Christ.

But, in India as elsewhere, the Church's best witness to Christ will be in the sphere, not of preaching, but of life.

(*a*) I have referred, in an earlier section of this chapter, to the witness which would be borne to Christ by a Church freed from racial pride and colour prejudice and exhibiting the marks of true brotherhood. Till this most eloquent of all preaching is effectively given, verbal preaching can have little effect.

The same may be said of all other kind of unity

in the Church. While the Church is divided into numerous sects, many of them in mutual rivalry and antagonism; while in certain parts of India what are virtually "caste churches" still exist; while there are factions among Christians of such bitterness that sometimes the members of two opposing parties cannot even worship together; the proclamation of the Gospel is of little avail.

The first essential change demanded by faithfulness to the teaching and spirit of Christ is the dawn of a new brotherhood, a new unity and love, in the Christian Church itself.

(*b*) Another such requirement is that the Indian Church should set itself to understand and practise in far fuller measure the life of prayer.

India has been pre-eminently, from the dawn of her history, a land of prayer. The great liturgical forms of worship, like the Vedic hymns; the rich treasuries of individual devotion; the prayers of the morning and evening Sandhya; the sacramental rites accompanying every chief event of life, from conception to the funeral pyre; the spiritual songs of poet-saints, and the meditations of sages; the rapt contemplation of *sadhus*, sitting for hours or days together in silent contact with the Eternal; the intercession of *rishis*, looking down from their watch-towers in the Himalayan heights upon the far-stretching plains of Hind and breathing out aspirations of love and blessing: what other land can show so all-pervading a sense as this of the place which man's conscious fellowship with God should take in his life's scheme?

Not without reason has it been said that the rest of the world may well sit at the feet of India to learn the secret of contemplation, the art of the mystic way.

Yet Christian saints and mystics need yield the palm to none in their practice of the life of prayer. There is no pathway of ascetic discipline, no way of prayer and contemplation, of mystical approach to God, which they have not explored. And one of the most poignant evidences of the failure of the Christian Church in India is that, with the example of Christ and His apostles before us, and with all the wealth of material which the lives and teachings of Christian mystics proffer at our disposal, we have so little impressed on Hindus the sense that we are men of prayer, that they hear with surprise and a new pleasure that Christianity also has its science of the mystic way.[1]

Here, then, is a task, most essential to its own spiritual life, most needful for effective witness and service, waiting for the Church in India in this new age—to explore the treasures of Christian prayer. Christian prayer has its own marked characteristics, distinguishing it from the prayers of other religions—characteristics naturally arising out of its central conception of God as Father. And, in spite of India's hoary wisdom in the things of the spirit, Christians, if only they will step apart a little from the crowded places and feverish activity

[1] It is sometimes asserted that the "mystical" element is lacking in Christ's own teaching about prayer; but this can only be maintained if the fourth Gospel is ruled out as entirely unhistorical.

of our modern life, and tarry in the silence with God, learning from the example of Christ Himself and from all the great Christian masters of the spiritual life, and practising with steadfast and quiet diligence, the life of prayer, Christians, too, will have their rich contribution to make to India's treasury of devotion and worship.

(*c*) One final illustration, and this the chief of all, of how we Christians in the new India must be true to the spirit of our Master. We must follow Him gladly and courageously in the royal way of the Cross, which is the Way of self-sacrificing love.

There must be no nigardliness in our spirit of service. Our Master came to be the servant of mankind. He came "not to be ministered unto but to minister, and to give His life a ransom for many." He taught that service is the only true greatness. He went about ceaselessly doing good. The life of active beneficence was for Him intertwined inextricably with the life of constant communion with God. That is the pattern which we must follow, if we are to be worthy of His name.

The service of the Indian Church will be, first and foremost, for India. It is the Motherland which must have the first claim. In the Christian ministry with all its manifold opportunities; in the public services of the country; in the legislative assemblies; in schools and colleges; in the work of industrial education and village uplift; in medicine and surgery; in nursing and maternity work; in sanitation and hygiene; in art and literature; in trade and commerce; in science and engineering; in agriculture and public works—Indian Christians will have unlimited scope for the service of the country. If they are true to the example of Christ, they will serve with no thought of reward and with the single motive of love; and they will be ready to endure with patience the hardships and difficulties which a life of faithful service entails.

But the service of the Indian Church will not be limited to India. The Church which Christ founded is an international body, and its outlook is as wide as humanity. The growth of the Indian Church has now reached a point at which it ought to be sending out workers to other lands. Mr. C. F. Andrews has repeatedly urged, for instance, that Indian Christians could do a work of great usefulness both for Indians and (still more) for Africans in Central Africa, if the Church there would avail itself of their help. Moreover, such service in other lands, demanding as it does a certain measure of enterprise and risk, would have a salutary influence on the Indian Church itself, enlarging its vision and quickening its spirit of sacrifice.

But, whether in India or in other lands, Indian Christians must be ready to offer their service without stint for the establishment of the reign of God in every walk of life. They must be ready, if need be, to follow so literally in the Way of the Cross as to give their very lives for this end.

In this work of establishing the Kingdom of God, Christians must look forward to co-operating, as far as may be, with those of other religions who are inspired by the same great ideal. As was pointed out by the Jerusalem Conference of 1929, the real conflict of the future will be not between one religion and another, but between the forces of religion and the forces of secularism. This is true of India as of other lands. It was pointed out in the first chapter of this book that, even though religion is so deeply rooted in India that we cannot believe it will be ever cast out, the secularist movement here also is not without its widespread influence. The powerful Youth Movement in the north of the country has made no secret of its conviction that the best thing for India would be the rooting out of all religion. The corresponding "Self-Respect Movement" of the south has followed the same line. A recent President of its conference who was very closely associated with Mahatma Gandhi in the Non-Co-operation Movement of 1921, said in the course of his address: "Men like Mahatma Gandhi may fast, and persons like Ganesh Shankar Vidyarthi may sacrifice their lives, but nonc of these remedies will successfully deal with the problem. It may be that some great men at a remote period in history have brought love in the name of religion, but nevertheless it cannot be disputed that the customs and practices associated with all religions to-day engender hatred between man and man. Religions thrive upon such divisions among the people. We of the Self-Respect Movement consider that mankind will attain liberty only when all religions are destroyed altogether."

Similarly, Mr. Paranjpye, who was formerly the Educational Minister of the Bombay Government, and is now a member of the India Council, is reported to have said: "Religion has been the bane of India; the sooner she gets rid of it, the better it will be for her." Many other evidences could be adduced of the same attitude.

In view of this assault upon religion, it is vital that all those who believe in God and in the supremacy of spiritual values, whatever be their creed, should regard themselves as allies rather than as foes, and seek out all possible ways in which, without surrendering their own distinctive convictions and principles, they may work together for the Kingdom of God. The International Fellowship, to which reference has been made above, is one of the most hopeful movements directed towards this end in India. It brings together Hindus, Moslems, Christians, Parsees, Jews and others on a basis of belief in God as the foundation for belief in human brotherhood; and, whilst insisting that each should follow his own convictions without compromise, is able to establish bonds of fellowship between the followers of the different religions such as make fruitful co-operation in a number of spheres possible.

If such conditions of friendly fellowship and co-operation between the members of the different faiths can be widely developed throughout India, it may do much to arrest the advance of secularism, and it will also enable Christians to play their part in an atmosphere of good will, unhindered by persecution or repression.

But we must face the possibility of a different alternative. In a most interesting paper on "the future of religion in the new India," an Indian

Christian of broad sympathies and wide experience writes:

> My own fear is that before long after India gets Swaraj, organized religious propaganda will be made illegal, and it is certain that such a measure will get general sympathy and support in the country. To me the passing of a law like this will be a terrible calamity.

He quotes the recent declaration of Mahatma Gandhi in *Young India*:

> If instead of confining themselves purely to humanitarian work such as education, medical services to the poor, and the like, they would use these activities of theirs for the purpose of proselytizing, I would certainly like them to withdraw. Every nation considers its own faith to be as good as that of any other. Certainly the great faiths held by the people of India are adequate for her people. India stands in no need of conversion from one faith to another.

And the comment on this of Mr. Natarajan, Editor of the *Indian Social Reformer*, "This is very much what the Reformer has been saying, and we are glad, in this as in many other matters, to find ourselves in agreement with him." The writer adds: "Last year (1930) in June or so, the *Indian Social Reformer* published a series of articles in which it pleaded that as soon as India got Swaraj, one of the first things to be done was to make all religious propaganda constitutionally and statutorily illegal."

The writer makes it clear that in his opinion the new Indian *raj* will be a "Hindu raj," and that it is not unlikely that such legislation against all religious propaganda may be passed.

It is certainly true that the characteristic Hindu

attitude is opposed to the attempt to change peoples' religious beliefs. Gandhi himself says that we ought not even in our thoughts to desire that a man of another faith should abandon that faith and accept our own. It is, therefore, not unlikely that a Hindu raj might desire to promulgate such anti-propaganda laws.

On the other hand, it has to be remembered that the religions of the two largest minority communities in India, the Moslems and the Christians, the former of whom are in some provinces in a majority, are essentially propagandist religions; and it seems unlikely that the new raj, even if predominantly Hindu, would wish to create disunion on an unparalleled scale in the country by antagonizing these two influential communities. Such action will be quite incompatible with modern conceptions of religious tolerance, such as that included in the Congress "Declaration of Rights," and it would gravely threaten the peaceful advance of the country, which depends upon securing the good will and co-operation of all its citizens. My own belief is that, whilst laws may be passed directed against *proselytizing*, in the sense of trying by compulsion and unworthy means to draw the members of one community to join another, it is unlikely that Government will hinder the peaceful and reasoned proclamation to others of what one believes to be the truth. Mahatma Gandhi's own amplification of his statement in *Young India* quoted above makes it clear that it is only unworthy methods of making converts which he really desires to make impossible.

"I am not against conversion," he says; "but I am against the modern methods of it. Conversion nowadays has become a matter of business, like any other. I remember having read a missionary report saying how much it cost per head to convert, and then presenting a budget for 'the next harvest.'" And again, "Religion after all is a deeply personal matter, it touches the heart. Why should I change my religion because a doctor who professes Christianity as his religion has cured me of some disease, or why should the doctor expect or suggest such a change whilst I am under his influence? Is not medical relief its own reward and satisfaction? Or why should I, whilst I am in a missionary educational institution, have Christian teaching thrust upon me? In my opinion these practices are not uplifting and give rise to suspicion if not even secret hostility. The methods of conversion must be like Cæsar's wife, above suspicion. Faith is not imparted like secular subjects. It is given through the language of the heart. If a man has a living faith in him, it spreads its aroma like the rose its scent. Because of its invisibility, the extent of its influence is far wider than that of the visible beauty of the colour of the petals."

It is clear from an article in the *Indian Social Reformer* of May 2, 1931, that Mr. Natarajan shares the opinion of Mahatma Gandhi, and is sure that no nationalist Indian Government will antagonize Indian Christians, but only oppose 'insidious ways of undermining another's faith."

But here all I am concerned to say is that, supposing in the new India legislation should be passed making *all* kinds of religious propaganda illegal, such action must make no difference to the Christians' attitude of loving and self-sacrificing service of the country. Christians would, of course, be bound to disobey the law: for they could only obey it by being untrue to their deepest convictions, and therefore becoming faithless and worthless servants of both God and of India. But in so disobeying they must have in their hearts no bitterness or resentment. Their Satyagraha must be the pure Satyagraha of love; so that, while they endure gladly for their convictions whatever sufferings are imposed upon them, they do so in the spirit of Christ's prayer for those who nailed Him to the Cross, seeking never to injure but only to win those who persecute them. They will realize that they can serve their country even by suffering; and they will suffer with joy at the hands of those they love.

There is a noble passage in the Early Christian "Epistle to Diognetus," belonging probably to the second century A.D., which illustrates well what the attitude of Christians amongst those who persecute them should be:

> Christians are not distinguished from the rest of mankind either in locality or in speech or in customs. For they dwell not somewhere in cities of their own, neither do they use some different language, nor practise an extraordinary kind of life. Nor again do they possess any invention discovered by any intelligence or study of ingenious men, nor are they masters of any human dogma as some are. But while they dwell in the cities of Greeks and barbarians

as the lot of each is cast, and follow the native customs in dress and food and the other arrangements of life, yet the constitution of their own citizenship, which they set forth, is marvellous, and confessedly contradicts expectation. They dwell in their own countries, but only as sojourners; they bear their share in all things as citizens, and they endure all hardships as strangers. Every foreign country is a fatherland to them, and every fatherland is foreign. . . . They find themselves in the flesh, and yet they live not after the flesh. Their existence is on earth, but their citizenship is in heaven. They obey the established laws and they surpass the laws in their own lives. They love all men and they are persecuted by all. They are ignored and yet they are condemned. They are put to death and yet they are endued with life. They are in beggary and yet they make many rich. They are in want of all things and yet they abound in all things. They are dishonoured and yet they are glorified in their dishonour. They are evil spoken of and yet they are vindicated. They are reviled, and they bless; they are insulted, and they respect. Doing good they are punished as evil doers; being punished they rejoice, as if they were thereby quickened by life.

If the Indian Church can live in the spirit of that early Christian ideal, she will not only gain her own soul, but she will do a mighty work of service in the new India, for which future generations will rise up and call her blessed.

INDEX